THE

ORIENTAL ANNUAL,

OR

Scenes in India;

COMPRISING

TWENTY-TWO ENGRAVINGS

FROM ORIGINAL DRAWINGS

BY WILLIAM DANIELL, R.A.

AND

A DESCRIPTIVE ACCOUNT

BY THE REV. HOBART CAUNTER, B.D.

LONDON:
BULL AND CHURTON, HOLLES STREET,
CAVENDISH SQUARE.
1835.

LONDON
PRINTED BY SAMUEL BENTLEY,
Dorset Street, Fleet Street

THIS VOLUME IS,

BY GRACIOUS PERMISSION,

DEDICATED TO THEIR ROYAL HIGHNESSES

THE DUCHESS OF KENT AND THE PRINCESS VICTORIA.

ADVERTISEMENT.

The great success of the ORIENTAL ANNUAL last year has encouraged the Proprietors to spare no expense to render the present volume still more worthy of public patronage.

Their object having been to make this work something beyond a mere elegant trifle, it will be found to contain matters of History and views of Society which they trust will render it a book for the Library as well as for the Drawing-room table.

In one respect the ORIENTAL ANNUAL differs from all works of a similar class;—it will be continued in yearly volumes, every three forming a distinct series.

The First Series will contain descriptions of the three English Presidencies:—the volume already published describes Madras:—the present volume describes Calcutta, and the third will describe Bombay.

ADVERTISEMENT.

Although no Series of the ORIENTAL ANNUAL will extend beyond three volumes, the work itself will be continued until the demand for it ceases. The materials, however, are so abundant and of such increasing interest, that it is confidently expected they will raise it each succeeding year still higher in public estimation.

September 20th, 1834.

ENGRAVINGS

FROM

𝔇𝔯𝔞𝔴𝔦𝔫𝔤𝔰

BY

WILLIAM DANIELL, ESQ. R.A.

INTERIOR OF A MOSQUE, JUANPORE (Frontispiece.)
INDIAN FRUIT-SELLER (Vignette Title.)
RHINOCEROS . . . . . . Page 4
YAK OF TIBET 28
THE SALAAM 52
AT NUJIBABAD, ROHILCUND 62
FAVOURITE OF THE HAREM . . . 80
MAUSOLEUM OF SUFTER JUNG . . . 96
THE AGRA GATE, CHAUTER SERAI . . . 106
MOSQUE AT MUTTRA 118
THE MOAH-PUNKEE AT LUCNOW . . . 128
MAUSOLEUM AT LUCNOW 138
THE RAJPOOTNI BRIDE 156
GARDEN OF THE PALACE, LUCNOW . . 172
THE BERNAR PAGODA, BENARES . . . 190
THE KUTWHUTTEA GATE, ROTAS GUR . . 210
TEMPLE AT MUDDUNPORE, BAHAR . . 222
GREAT TEMPLE AT BODE GYAH . . . 232
MOSQUE IN THE COIMBATORE . . . 234
KUTWALLEE GATE, GOUR 244
CALCUTTA, FROM GARDEN-HOUSE REACH . 254
BOA CONSTRICTOR AND BOAT'S CREW . . 260

SCENES IN INDIA.

CHAPTER I.

SINGULAR TEMPLE.—THE RHINOCEROS.—SERINAGUR.

Upon quitting Hurdwar, as I have stated in the conclusion of the former volume, we proceeded towards the mountains. A short distance from that venerated spot where ablutions in the Ganges are considered so especially efficacious to spiritual purgation, there is a remarkable banyan tree. It is consecrated to the worship of the Hindoo godhead, and its sanctuary is constantly visited by devout pilgrims from the neighbouring countries. The stem, of vast circumference, is surrounded by a terrace. It is hollowed out into a chamber of considerable dimensions, which has been converted into a temple by the pious zeal of the devotees who visit it daily, merely entering on one side and passing out at the other, where they pay tribute, after the manner of all true believers, in the current mintage of the land; by which they acquire a mystical purification. Being aliens from the privileged stock, we were not allowed to enter the adytum of this forest sanctuary, lest we should desecrate its hallowed mysteries and thus neutralize the potential efficacy with which the presiding deity is supposed to have endowed it. Immediately beyond are several small temples devoted to the mysteries of Hindoo superstition; and as the population in this neighbourhood is chiefly composed of the poorer and more ignorant classes which are invariably the dupes of their priests, the services of their temples here exhibit all the absurdities of idolatry without any of its less revolting features. This is evidently a place of more than ordinary sanctity. There is an air of solemnity, almost of solitariness about it that renders it unusually imposing, bounded as it appears to be by the neighbouring mountains which project their huge shadows over it.

The ministering Bramins relate strange stories of this marvellous tree, to them an object at once of profit and of superstition, assigning to it an existence anterior to the deluge; and they enumerate a greater number of souls as having been saved by passing through it than the world has contained since the period of that awful visitation. There is nothing remarkable in the upper growth of the tree, which does not cover so large a space as some others on the banks of the Ganges; and though the trunk is tolerably vigorous and has the remnant of a long life apparently yet before it, still does it exhibit evident symptoms of having passed the vigour of its time. The withering grasp of decay has already fixed upon it.

We entered the mountains by the Coaduwar ghaut, meeting several travellers, who gave us the rather discouraging information that the snow had begun to fall before they left Serinagur, where it was our intention to make our final halt. As we advanced, the sky appeared to be tinged with a deep dingy red, and, upon suddenly emerging from a narrow glen, to our astonishment the distant mountains seemed to be in a blaze. The fire swept up their sides to the extent of several miles, undulating like the agitated waves of the ocean when reddened by the slanting beams of the setting sun. It was like an ignited sea, exhibiting an effect at once new and fearful.

This striking phenomenon is not by any means uncommon and is accounted for by the larger bamboos, as they are swayed by the wind, emitting fire from their hard glossy stems through the violence of their friction, and thus spreading destruction through the mountain forests. These are so extensive that the fire continues to burn for many days together, and is often as suddenly extinguished as it is ignited by those mighty deluges of rain, so common in mountainous countries, where the water pours from the clouds in confluent masses resembling small cataracts, and in a few moments arrests the progress of a still more formidable element. No one can form a conception of the violence of the torrents which occasionally fall on these mountains, from anything that has been witnessed in the more temperate latitudes of the opposite hemisphere. Here indeed, when they do fall, to use the sublime imagery of the Jewish lawgiver, " the windows of heaven appear to be opened." It is scarcely possible for man or beast to stand against the impetuosity of their descent. Every living thing seeks the shelter of the forests where immense trees, the growth of ages, afford but an imperfect protection.

These forests, which cover the bases of the hills, are filled with all kinds of game, especially pea-fowl, and it is a beautiful sight to behold those splendid birds come at sunrise from the deep recesses of the woods, as they do in large flocks, and completely cover the valleys. The wild elephant is found in the lower regions of the mountains, and so is the rhinoceros, though less frequently. Of the latter animal we were fortunate enough to obtain a view, which is by no means a usual thing, as it is not gregarious like the elephant, and therefore much more rarely met with. We had turned the angle of a hill that abutted upon a narrow stream, when, on the opposite side of the rivulet, we saw a fine male rhinoceros; it was standing near the edge of the water with its head slightly bent, as if it had been just slaking its thirst in the cooling stream. It stood, apparently with great composure, about two hundred yards above us, in an open vista of the wood. Mr. Daniell, under the protection of a lofty intervening bank, was able to approach sufficiently near to make a perfect sketch of it; after which, upon a gun being fired, it deliberately walked off into the jungle. It did **not** appear in the least intimidated at the sight of our party, which remained at some distance, nor at all excited by the discharge of the gun.

There are two species of this animal, the bicornis and the unicornis; the latter supposed to be the unicorn of scripture. The former is, I believe, peculiar to Africa: it is never known in India, where the one-horned rhinoceros alone is found. Its size is only inferior to that of the elephant, although it is considerably smaller. Its bulk, however, is greater in proportion to its height, and, from its superior courage and activity, it is a much more formidable creature. Its head resembles that of a pig, and it has two small dull eyes which give it an appearance at once stupid and intractable. Its length, not including the tail, is from eleven to twelve feet, and the circumference of its body about the same; though it is said sometimes to exceed this standard. It occasionally attains to the height of seven feet, and is amazingly strong, while its skin is so hard and thick as to be generally impervious to a musket ball. The hide is curiously divided into sections, and the different divisions are adapted with such exquisite precision as to have the appearance, at a short distance, of a beautiful coat of mail. It is extremely rough, and offers so complete a resistance to the touch, as not to yield in the slightest degree to the strongest pressure. The only vulnerable parts are the belly, the eyes, and near the ears.

This animal is of very sequestered habits; it traverses the most impenetrable jungles alone and is the terror of every creature with which it comes in contact, although it seldom attacks unless provoked by aggression. The horn upon its nose, which is thick and pointed, curves upwards towards the forehead, forming an acute angle with the bone of the snout, and projecting from it about thirty inches. It is a most fearful weapon; so much so, that even the colossal elephant has been occasionally laid prostrate by a well

directed stroke from the armed head of this terrible adversary. The horn does not adhere to the bone, but when the animal is in its ordinary state, stands loose between the nostrils; the moment, however, that the rhinoceros is excited to resistance by the approach or attack of a foe, the muscular tension is so great that the horn instantly becomes immovably fixed, and he is able to dart it into the trunk of a tree to the depth of several inches.

The upper lip of this animal is of great length and remarkably pliant, acting like a short proboscis, by which he grasps the roots of trees and other esculent substances, and it is capable of contraction or expansion as circumstances may require. "With this lip," says Bruce, "and the assistance of his tongue, he pulls down the upper branches which have most leaves, and these he devours first. Having stripped the tree of its branches, he does not directly abandon it, but, placing his snout as low in the trunk as he finds his horn will enter, he rips up the body of the tree and reduces it to thin pieces like so many laths; and when he has thus prepared it, he embraces as much as he can of it in his monstrous jaws and twists it round with as much ease as an ox would do a root of celery."

The female generally produces only a single young one at a birth, which attains to a full state of maturity in about fifteen years. The rhinoceros is of a savage disposition and seems to exist merely to gratify a voracious appetite. When excited, it displays paroxysms of fury which render it highly dangerous for any one to approach. As it is of a temper much less mild than the elephant, it is far more formidable when exasperated, on account of its greater activity and more desperate ferocity. The voraciousness of this creature is extraordinary: it will consume as much as an elephant. A young one, only two years old, sent from Bengal in 1739, cost a thousand pounds sterling for food, including the expenses of its passage.

Before we entered the pass of the mountains which separates them from the plains, we were obliged to obtain permission from the Rajah of Serinagur to visit his capital. This permission was readily granted, though it caused some delay, as the formalities even of a petty Rajah's court are invariably more numerous than agreeable; we nevertheless contrived to spend the intervening time pleasantly enough in the valleys through which our route lay to the Coaduwar Ghaut. The Rajah sent an escort with two hirkarrahs* to conduct us from this place, where the mountains began to close in upon our path, exhibiting to our view that grandeur of form and majesty of aspect for which this mighty range is so preeminently distinguished. At this pass, upon the summit of a tabular hill which is ascended by steps cut in the rock, is built a small neat village, flanked by a strong barrier and gateway. The walls on either side the portal are very massy and the entrance narrow. The valley by which the hill is immediately bounded is protected towards the plains by a rapid stream, which taking a circular direction nearly encloses it on two sides, rushing down into the lower

---

* A hirkarrah is a messenger.

valleys with a din and turbulence peculiar to mountain torrents.

The gate of the village was guarded by a small detachment of the Rajah's troops, and on passing under its low arch we entered the territory of Serinagur. This village is quite deserted during the rainy season, when the ghaut is rendered altogether impassable and becomes the abode of tigers, leopards, bears, hyenas, and other beasts of prey, which retire into the jungles as soon as clearer skies and a more genial temperature invite the return of man. Here the vakeel,* sent by the Rajah, procured for us the necessary number of diggeries and sillenies — the former to bear our palankeens, the latter to carry our baggage; he was exceedingly civil and showed every disposition to diminish the difficulties which invariably arise to impede the progress of the mountain traveller. In these mountains especially there is generally a reluctance in the natives to contribute to the accommodation of a stranger, and it is no easy matter, at any time, to obtain porters to transport his baggage. They are for the most part a very indolent race, although accustomed to encounter the severities of want and to undergo occasionally the most difficult and arduous labours.

The palankeen used in these hills is of a peculiar construction and admirably adapted to the asperities of the region. In the precipitous ascents which here continually occur, the path frequently winds round angles so abrupt and acute, that it would

* The vakeel is literally an ambassador.

be impossible to get round them with the ordinary palankeen; the poles, therefore, of those which are adapted to mountain journeys are divided in the centre, acting upon a movable hinge, opening before and behind the palenkeen as the front bearer turns the sharp angle of a hill, and resuming their original position as soon as the abutment has been cleared and the path again becomes straight. It is wonderful to see with what agility the sillenies scale the steep acclivities, where there often appears scarcely footing for a goat, with loads that would distress any person of ordinary strength even upon level ground: they carry with them bamboos crossed at the top by a short transverse stick in the form of the ancient Greek T, upon which they rest their loads when fatigued. They are generally small men, but their limbs are large and the muscles strongly developed, from the severe exercise to which their laborious employment subjects them. Their legs are frequently disfigured by varicose veins which dilate to the size of a man's little finger, appearing like cords twisted round their limbs and causing in the spectator a somewhat painful feeling of apprehension lest they should suddenly burst,—a consequence that could not fail to be fatal.

We found the road here to be difficult and frequently dangerous, winding along the edges of deep ravines and occasionally cut through the solid surface of the rock. The waters of the Coah Nullah dashed beneath our path over their narrow rocky bed, foaming and hissing on their way to the parent stream, of which they formed one of the numerous accessories.

The channel is occasionally almost choked with huge masses of rock, which fall from the beetling precipices above and so interrupt the course of the stream that it boils and lashes over them with an uproar truly appalling; especially when the traveller casts his anxious eye upon it while crossing one of those frail bridges over which he is so frequently obliged to pass in a journey through these mountains.

We again met with some delay, in consequence of the alarm of our servants at the aspect of the country. Many of them refused to advance, and, notwithstanding the civility of the Rajah's vakeel in procuring us porters, several of these quitted us shortly after we left the Coaduwar ghaut, and we had great difficulty in supplying their places; and when this was finally accomplished, it was not without resorting to a compulsory mode of discipline which necessity only could have warranted but against which there was no alternative. Thus we were obliged to obtain by stripes what we could not do by persuasion. We, however, at length procured the number required, over whom a vigilant watch was kept as we proceeded.

During our halt a circumstance occurred which I confess I feel no little pleasure at having the opportunity of recording, as it is highly characteristic of the skill of these mountaineers in baffling the ferocious propensities of those animals by which they are so perpetually threatened with mischief. I had entered a deep dell with my gun, accompanied by two hillmen, in order to try if I could not succeed in killing some jungle-fowl which are here tolerably abundant, though so wild as to render it a matter of no common difficulty to get near them. After a long and fatiguing walk, we ascended with some toil a very sudden abruption of the mountain, when upon gaining the summit, which overhung a precipice, a bear started from a recess in the neighbouring covert and advanced evidently with sinister intentions towards us. I was about to fire, though my gun was only loaded with large shot, when one of my highland guides motioned to me to desist, giving me to understand, by significant gesticulations (for I understood his language but very indifferently) that he would attack the enemy unarmed; and from the coolness and dexterity with which he commenced operations, I confess I could not persuade myself to doubt of a favourable result, in spite of the difficulties which seemed to defy its accomplishment. Almost upon the extreme edge of the precipice stood a tall tree with strong vertical branches, apparently of the character though not the form of the mountain-ash, being very tough and elastic. The hill-man approached the bear and by exciting it withdrew its attention from me towards himself. The exasperated beast immediately made him the object of attack, when the man adroitly sprang on the tree, as nimbly followed by the bear. The former having reached the upper branches, he quickly slipped a strong cord over the top of the limb upon which he stood, at the same time dropping the reverse end upon the ground. This was instantly seized by his companion, who, pulling with all his strength, drew the point of the bough downward until the branch projected nearly in a horizontal line from the stem: there were no intervening branches betwixt this and the precipice, the edge of which it nearly overhung when in its natural position. As soon as the bough was warped to the necessary degree of tension, the mountaineer crept cautiously as near the extremity as he could with safety, followed as cautiously by the bear; but, the moment he saw his angry foe upon the bent branch, he dexterously let himself down by the cord to the ground. The bear, thus unexpectedly deprived of its victim, attempted to turn, in order to retrace its steps; no sooner however had it relaxed its grasp of the bough for this purpose, than the hill-man suddenly cut the cord, which had been securely tied to the stump of a tree, and the depressed branch instantly gained its original position with an irresistible momentum. The suddenness and vigour of the recoil shook the bear from its hold, elancing it, like the fragment of a rock from a catapult, into the empty air; uttering a stifled yell, it was hurled over the precipice, and, falling with a dull crash upon the rocks beneath, no doubt soon became a prey to the vultures and jackals. The address with which the bold highlander accomplished this dangerous exploit was as astonishing as it was novel.

In the course of our progress towards Serinagur, we found all kinds of European trees and plants in abundance. We saw sweet-briar, with and without thorns; walnut, maple, and willow-trees; apple and pear, peach, apricot, and barberry-trees; birch, yew, beech, pine, ash, and fir-trees: we saw likewise the mulberry, laurel, hazel, and marsh-mallow. Raspberries, strawberries, and gooseberries, abound in this region, and flowers with which every European is familiar, the dog-rose, heliotrope, hollyhock, marigold, nasturtium, poppy, larkspur; lettuces, turnips, cabbages, and potatoes, are also very plentiful—indeed, I think there is scarcely a European fruit, flower, or esculent vegetable, that is not to be found in some part or other of these mountains. We were told that oaks were occasionally seen in the higher regions of this immense chain, though we did not happen to see any. The common stinging-nettle was very abundant, though somewhat more potent in its powers of infliction than the same plant so well known in Europe; and it was truly amusing to see with what alacrity one or two Bengalee servants who had ventured to accompany us, having unwittingly squatted down upon a tuft of these insidious evergreens, sprang upon their feet, gaping with inquisitive surprise at the cause of their sudden celerity.

As we advanced, we crossed several nullahs in which were huge disjointed masses that had fallen from the superincumbent rocks, so rounded and polished by constant attrition—for the extreme agitation of the waters produced a perpetual whirlpool—that one might have imagined they had been submitted to the process of human labour. During the rains, by which the torrents are immensely swelled, their agitation is inconceivably violent; in fact, the impetus of the stream is then so great, that stones of immense magnitude are washed from the mountains and precipitated into the plains below.

By this time the difficulties of our route had considerably increased: to look down some of the gaping gulfs which arrested our gaze as we passed them, required no ordinary steadiness of brain, and the road by which we had to descend was frequently so steep that we were obliged to cling to the jagged projections of rock or to the few stunted shrubs that appeared here and there in our path in spite of the asperity of the stony surface through which they with difficulty forced their way. The prospect between those lofty eminences which every now and then rose in solemn grandeur before us, was sublime beyond conception: glens so dark and deep that the powers of vision were baffled by their profundity, and the tall spires which towered majestically above them, hooded by light feathery clouds, presenting a contrast at once the grandest and most picturesque, exhibited altogether a scene of singular and wild magnificence. So awful is the impression made by these stupendous objects, that, were it not for the occasional relief afforded by the gentler livery of vegetation which sometimes so beautifully displays itself on these gigantic hills, the traveller would find it almost impossible to proceed. Impediments began now to multiply upon us: we were obliged occasionally to wade through the nullahs as high as our hips, and found it no easy matter to keep our footing on account of the impetuous rushing of the waters, while the circular stones with which their channels abounded rendered them generally anything but easy to pass over. It is scarcely possible to imagine the difficulty of crossing these mountain-streamlets, and this is much increased by the danger; the least slip would be attended with imminent peril, for such is the force of the torrents, that if the whole attention and strength of the traveller were not employed, they would bear him off his legs, and, once swept from his footing, there would be scarcely a chance of saving him, for he would be hurried over a number of low but dangerous falls and dashed against the rocks beneath. The beds of these nullahs are very irregular, and, though narrow, are generally deep, while the number of smooth stones which have accumulated in them render the footing so slippery as to require great circumspection in order to secure a safe transit. One of our followers was struck down by the impetuosity of the waters, and was only saved by catching hold of the branch of a tree that had fortunately fallen across the stream. The roar of the torrents when swollen by the rains is so loud, that you can scarcely hear your own voice in their vicinity, and, multiplied as it is by the repercussion of the surrounding hills, it produces an unintermitting confusion of sounds as disagreeable as they are stunning. Our ascent was at times so painfully laborious that we scarcely advanced more than half a mile in an hour. We pursued our journey in silence and in weariness—there was not a smile upon a single countenance; on the contrary, the features of every one bore an expression of deep solemnity.

It is surprising with what an imperturbable gravity the traveller generally pursues his alpine journey; he is affected by far different feelings when scaling precipices, than when he is quietly traversing the plains As he climbs those mighty steeps which appear as if they were the pillars of the world he dwells in, the deepest emotions are awakened; there is an awe inspired by the grandeur of the scene around him of which he cannot divest himself, for he seems to feel as if he were in immediate communication with the mysterious agents of the universe. He here, with a subdued but gushing heart, "looks through nature" in her most stupendous sublimities "up to nature's God," beholding him in the glorious works by which he is himself surrounded, and feeling at once that he is indeed a God infinite in wisdom and unapproachable in his omnipotence. Every sentiment seems to converge into one focus, every mental association is of one tone and complexion—in short, the whole mind becomes rapt in one absorbing feeling of veneration.

We passed several villages as we advanced towards Serinagur in which the houses were tolerably well constructed, though huddled together without either order or uniformity; they were, however, upon the whole, not deficient in accommodation. As in Savoy and I believe in mountainous regions generally, so in these mountains, the side of the hill commonly forms one of the walls of the highlander's tenement, against which the roof is fixed and supported by two strong stone walls projecting at right angles from the face of the hill; the area being closed in by a third wall completing the square. These houses are entered by a low doorway, through which the inmates are obliged to creep, the aperture not being high enough to admit a child of more than three years old without stooping.

Our road now lay up a very precipitous mountain, the bleak sides of which had been bared of vegetation by one of those conflagrations already noticed and not uncommon in these regions. The charred stumps of trees were everywhere visible as we ascended, presenting an aspect at once of ruin and desolation by no means cheering; higher up, however, the jungle remained entire. After slowly winding for some distance between two hills, we entered a dense thicket which day appeared never to have visited, for it was involved in a perpetual twilight: the sun seemed never to have penetrated its deep and gloomy recesses. Though we could distinguish no distant objects we could still hear the roar of the cataract; it brawled hoarsely through the blast, which interrupted only to bring it to the ear with more fearful indistinctness.

We now commenced a rapid and difficult descent; it led us into a valley overhung by the peaks of mountains which seemed to plunge their tall spires into the skies and absolutely to prop the firmament. Here, on the bare and scarped sides of the precipice above, pine-trees blasted or riven by the lightning rattled their seared trunks in the wind, which, moaning through them in low hollow gusts, seemed to a saddened spirit like the wailing of the dead. Looking at the sky from this dismal valley, as if from the interior of a huge funnel, the stars were visible as shining through a pall. The heavens appeared to be one uniform tint of the deepest purple, whilst the brilliancy with which the stars emitted their vivid fires altogether baffles description; they shone intensely bright, and, although it at least wanted two hours of sunset, night seemed already to have established its supremacy. Nothing could exceed the splendour of the scene.

Emerging from this valley, we commenced another arduous ascent, and although the summit of the hill appeared to promise a cessation of our labours, yet we had no sooner surmounted it than other hills rose before us, thus presenting to our view an interminable succession of difficulties.

> So pleased at first, the towering Alps we try,
> Mount o'er the vales, and seem to tread the sky,
> The eternal snows appear already past,
> And the first clouds and mountains seem the last;
> But, those attain'd, we tremble to survey
> The growing labours of the lengthen'd way,
> The increasing prospect tires our wondering eyes,
> Hills peep o'er hills, and alps on alps arise.

CHAPTER II.

A THUNDERSTORM.—GOITRES.—AN ELK SHOT.

The third day after our departure from the Coaduwar ghaut we encountered a storm of thunder and lightning such as can never be easily effaced from my memory. On the morning of this day we had observed that the motion of the clouds gradually increased, the fleecy masses occasionally meeting and variously blending with the sunbeams, from which they reflected a great variety of beautiful tints; thus imparting an agreeable colouring to the surrounding landscape. The sky was bright above us, though the atmosphere was sultry and oppressive. The rack at length spread over the hills, skimming rapidly along their precipitous sides and occasionally rolling in undulating volumes, deepening as it expanded upon their bare or shaggy tops and assuming forms the most singular and fantastic. In the course of a few minutes after we had observed this hurried gathering of the clouds, without any further indication, the sky became suddenly overcast, involving us in a gloom so intense as to render every object within a few yards of us perfectly indistinct. The rain quickly poured down upon us in a deluge. We contrived to obtain a tolerable shelter under a projecting ledge which overhung a part of our path to the extent of several feet. The lightning streamed from the clouds as from a mighty reservoir, wrapping the whole mountains in flame, and literally, in the words of Scripture, " ran along the ground." The flashes were so quick in succession that there was only the pause of a few seconds between them, while the peals of thunder which followed were almost deafening. The scene was grand beyond description. The loud and successive peals were multiplied to such a degree by the surrounding echoes, that there was one continued and tremendous crash of several minutes, and at the first pause the silence was so intense as to be positively painful. The thunder was repeated from rock to rock, rolling along the valleys as if subverting the very bases of the hills, and finally hushing its portentous roar in those interminable glens where the eye cannot penetrate and even the contemplation of which causes the brain to whirl. Though the storm did not continue above a few minutes, it was nevertheless some time before we entirely recovered from its effects; it had, indeed, made a deep impression on us all and was by far the most terrible, for the time it lasted, I had ever witnessed. The atmosphere now quickly brightened; the clouds separated before the sun which threw a clear flood of light upon the dripping foliage whence it was cast back in numberless vivid reflections, while the retreating thunders were heard only at a distance and after long intervals. The heavy masses of vapour which had enveloped the mountains shortly dispersed and there soon appeared not a vestige of the late storm.

Evening was now approaching and its shades were already beginning to deepen upon the surrounding landscape. Before we had proceeded far, the setting sun in his descent assumed a fiery glow that tinged with the same vivid hue every object from which his beams were reflected. The clouds which had gathered on the horizon opened before his track, and through the interval his rays streamed with the most dazzling intensity: they were arrested by the tops of the mountains and even the dark glens beneath caught a portion of their departing radiance. The whole prospect was for the moment brilliantly irradiated by the same fiery beam. We were surrounded by mountains that towered above each other to a prodigious altitude, while the effect of the deep glow of the setting sun upon these gigantic objects, contrasted with the clear placid light of the snowy range, which was distinctly visible, was as striking as it was beautiful.

Indra, god of the elements, is a deity highly venerated in these hills. The various transformations of this Hindoo Jupiter are related with great gravity by the mountaineers. He is one of the chief heroes of their mythology; and where hurricanes are so frequent, no wonder, according to their creed at least, that he

" Who guides the whirlwind and directs the storm"

should be an object of especial veneration. One of his incarnations is beautifully alluded to by Sir William Jones in his spirited hymn.

" The reckless peasant who these glowing flowers,
   Hopeful of rubied fruit, had fostered long,
   Seized and with cordage strong
Shackled the god * who gave him showers.
Straight from seven winds immortal genii flew.
   Varuna green, whom foamy waves obey;
   Bright Vahni, flaming like the lamp of day;
Kuvera, sought by all, enjoyed by few;
   Marut, who bids the winged breezes play;
   Stern Yama, ruthless judge! and Isa cold,
   With Nairrit, mildly bold:—
They, with the ruddy flash that points the thunder,
Rend his vain bands asunder.
Th' exulting god resumes his thousand eyes,
Four arms divine, and robes of changing dyes."

We had now advanced sufficiently far into the hills, to witness one of the most grievous inflictions to which the inhabitants of all mountainous districts are subject. That huge wen known in the Swiss alps under the name of goitre is here even more prevalent; it enlarges to an immense size, often entirely encircling the neck, and giving an aspect of the most revolting deformity to those miserable creatures who are the objects of this dreadful visitation. Some of these tumours were of such enormous dimensions as to force the head considerably backward, at the same time reaching nearly to the breast, while the sickly hue of the complexion, and the squalid appearance altogether of those thus afflicted, excited an emotion of disgust at once painful and irrepressible.

* Indra assumed the form of a shepherd-boy, and entering a garden to steal pomegranate-blossoms for his beloved Indrani, was seized and bound by the owner. This legend will remind the classical reader of Ovid's account of Bacchus bound by the sailors. Met. lib. iii.

These frightful excrescences are sometimes removed with the knife by the native surgeons, who are much more unskilful than the commonest farrier in Europe; they mangle dreadfully the patient upon whom they operate, but it is astonishing how soon he recovers, in consequence of the pure state of his blood arising from the simplicity of his diet. So free are these people from a feverish habit of body that after the loss of a limb, which is removed by a most clumsy and summary process, a poultice of turmeric combined with a few herbs is applied, which occasions a gradual suppuration and thus the stump heals in an incredibly short space of time.

Early in the afternoon of this day we came to a rude bridge which it was necessary to cross in order to save a circuit of several miles. This we determined to do, in spite of the hazard which is by no means trifling to one unaccustomed to so novel a method of transportation. The bridge consisted simply of two ropes of about an inch and half in diameter made of twisted creepers, eighteen inches apart, passed through a hoop and secured on either side of the stream by strong bamboos driven firmly into the earth parallel to each other. The passenger places himself between the parallel ropes within the hoop, on the lower rim of which he is seated, and, holding a rope in either hand, pulls himself across. To the hill-men this is a sufficiently easy process and they perform it without the slightest apprehension; but to any one who has never before trusted himself upon such an equivocal machine, over a deep and impetuous torrent at an elevation of from eighty to a hundred feet, it is a matter of no ordinary peril. Nothing can be well conceived more appalling than, hanging over the tremendous abyss supported by two small ropes and a hoop, to cast the eye down upon the hissing flood beneath, tossed and agitated into innumerable whirlpools by the narrowness and asperity of the channel, the whole machine fearfully vibrating and threatening to give way at every impulse of the wind, which frequently whistles over the trembling passenger with most menacing violence.

We had scarcely reached the opposite side in safety, when a fine elk started from a thick grove of trees on the hill side, and was shot by two of our attendants armed with matchlocks. This is the animal known under the more generic name of the moose-deer. It is an inhabitant, I believe, of the four continents, though always found in hilly countries. Its habits are gentle, and it is so timid that, when first started from its covert, overcome by fear, it will fall upon its knees and remain in that position for several seconds, thus giving the hunter an opportunity of easily securing his prey. But if this opportunity be lost, the vigorous animal darts forward with a speed scarcely credible, defying all pursuit, and thus continues without the least diminution of its progress to the distance of many leagues. Though of the gentlest character, it will defend itself with great energy when attacked, using its horns with a dexterity that baffles the approach of dogs, which it gores or strikes with its forefeet with such force as frequently to lay them dead upon the spot. It is usually about the size of a common English ox.

After a short progress we reached a chasm, above

which the mountain rose to an immense altitude, and we had to ascend its steep sides by a path so narrow as only to admit one passenger in line. A broad cataract bounded over the precipice, up the side of which we were ascending. Just as we had reached the summit, one of the sillenies dropped from his shoulder a small portmanteau which fell into the gulf below. He expressed his determination to recover it by descending, although the depth was at least two hundred feet, and accordingly prepared to accomplish his resolution. A stout cord, composed of hair, was passed round the limb of a tree that projected over the precipice. The end was firmly tied to a thick bamboo, about fifteen inches long, upon which the man placed his feet, and, grasping the rope in both hands, was slowly lowered into the void. As the face of the precipice sloped gradually inward, he was not within reach of it during the whole of his descent. When about fifty yards below the summit, he was swayed in an alarming degree by the wind, which, pouring down into the chasm and not finding a ready vent, was forced back again in strong eddies that seemed at times to whirl him round with dangerous velocity. He, however, still maintained his hold until he appeared but a speck, when the cord slackening, it was clear that he had reached his destination. After a short time, upon a signal being given from below by a sudden jerk of the cord, the men above began to haul up their companion, who, from the additional weight, had evidently recovered his burden. They pulled him up much more expeditiously than they had let him down, and he soon appeared uninjured with the portmanteau upon his shoulders.

On the sixth day after we quitted Hurdwar, we entered Serinagur. During the whole march of the preceding day the snowy range had been distinctly visible, looking like a white drapery hanging from the skies over the blue tops of the distant mountains. It seemed perfectly detached from the hills, above which it rose to an elevation that appeared to blend it with the heavens, whilst its surface of unsullied whiteness, catching the rays of the sun, reached the eye through the distance, softened into a purity of effect that carried the imagination to a world unknown to man, of which it seemed to form a part. The impression conveyed by a scene at once so novel and imposing, was solemn in the extreme.

Shortly after our arrival at Serinagur, we were introduced to the Rajah. We found him an intelligent person, courteous in his manners, and of easy, unembarrassed address. His countenance indicated no peculiar trait of character, yet was by no means deficient in intelligence. His manners inspired confidence and he received us with an undissembled welcome. He was frank and free, though somewhat effeminate, giving great attention to his dress which was evidently arranged with extreme care. He wore large gold bangles on his wrists, while his fingers were covered with rings of different shapes and weight, composed of the same metal.

The inhabitants of Serinagur appear to be a mixed race, exhibiting in their features the blended lineaments of highlander, lowlander, Patan, Tartar, Chinese, and Hindoo; and often showing the especial peculiarities of those several races. Their complexions are swarthy, though in a slight degree, and they have very little beard; yet when they possess more than the usual superfluity it is a good deal prized by them. They are, upon the whole, a mild, inoffensive race, and though not deficient in courage to make resistance when attacked, they have displayed very little ingenuity in devising the most effectual means of defence, considering the advantages which their mountains afford them.

On the second day after our arrival the Rajah paid us a visit in form, accompanied by the principal officers of his court. There was, however, very little ceremony observed upon what might be considered a state occasion,—for he came in full court costume. At our first visit we had presented him with a pair of pistols and a watch; the latter he now brought with him, requesting us to explain how it performed its movements and how the different divisions of the day were indicated on the dial, as he had never before seen such a machine, although he had heard its powers extolled by those who had descended into the plains and there held intercourse with Europeans. He was highly gratified when made thoroughly to comprehend the complicated structure of the watch, and this he readily did, for he was by no means slow of comprehension. Indeed, a quickness of perception is a general characteristic of the Hindoo of every denomination. I do not think that the mental qualities of this highly gifted people have been hitherto sufficiently appreciated. Their superstitions have too frequently been the mask through which their intellectual features have been scrutinized, and this medium has deformed them instead of presenting a faithful delineation.

After the powers of the watch had been explained to the Rajah, a little gunpowder was presented to him, with the strength of which he seemed surprised, as that made by the natives is far less efficacious than the powder manufactured in Europe. A charge was put into the hands of his gun-bearer to load his master's matchlock with, but the man smiled at the smallness of the quantity and insisted upon doubling it. He did so and the result was a recoil that instantly laid him on his back, almost dislocated his shoulder and so damaged the matchlock that he was obliged to put it into the hands of an armourer. The astonished servitor was now experimentally convinced that the strength of the powder had not been exaggerated; though he confessed it with a very rueful countenance. He affected, however, to treat the matter lightly, but the rigidity of his smile betrayed the counterfeit, while the grin upon the features of the bystanders showed that they had little sympathy for his misfortune. The Rajah was a good deal amused at the issue of his servant's obstinacy, and we shortly after parted with mutual expressions of kindness and good wishes.

Before we quitted Serinagur we visited the Rajah's stable, in which was a beautiful animal of the bovine species, called a yak. It is the domestic bull of Tibet. I do not believe that a single specimen of this creature now exists in Europe. In Tibet it is found both in the wild and tame state, though chiefly in the latter. As the wealth of the Tartar hordes consists principally in their cattle, they have large herds.

These are their most valuable property, for they live almost entirely upon the milk. They sell the hair of the yak to great advantage, as it is in much request throughout the countries immediately around them.

This animal is about five feet high and has much the form and bulk of a common English bull. The chief point of dissimilarity between the yak and every other animal of this genus consists in its sides being covered with long glossy hair which extends over the whole body, except the head and legs, and hangs from the flanks quite down to the hocks. The head is not so long as that of the English bull and the ears are smaller. The horns are of greater length, tapering from the skull to the extremities, and forming a horizontal arch; they gradually incline towards each other until near the end, when they make a sudden curve upwards. The forehead seems to protrude considerably, but this is probably owing to a thick tuft of curly hair which traverses it, partly shading the eyes, and giving rather a heavy expression to the animal's features. The eyes are large, though not bright, and project boldly from the sockets, without however conveying the disagreeable impression which a projecting eye-ball is apt to create; as the hair of the forehead neutralizes the unfavourable effect.

The yak has all the genuine marks of high breeding and unmixed blood. The nostrils are small but open, the nose is also small and delicately shaped, presenting likewise that roundness and smoothness of surface so common to animals of a pure breed. The neck

is short but arched; and, as in the Brahminee bull, peculiar to Hindostan, there is a high hump between the shoulders: this is coated with a profusion of short curly hair, extremely soft and of a texture very different from that which covers the other parts of the body. This soft fur, for such it really is, overspreads the shoulders, and continues, though in less profusion, along the back, extending to the root of the tail, which is composed of an immense tuft of long bright hair that almost sweeps the ground, and adds greatly to the elegance of this singularly beautiful animal. It is far more copious than the tail of the largest English cart-horse; not so long, indeed, but much thicker, while the hair is finer and more glossy, entirely enveloping the tail, and is as great an ornament to this fine creature as a luxuriant head of hair to a handsome woman. In some of these bulls it is perfectly white, every other part of the animal being quite black, except the soft fur which covers the shoulders, hump, and spine. This order is frequently reversed, though occasionally the colours vary considerably; but black with white, as seen in the accompanying engraving, is the most prevailing order, and I think the most striking.

The legs of the yak are very short, while the body appears disproportionably large from the profusion of hair with which it is overspread. On some of these animals this is so long as to trail upon the ground, which gives an ungainly appearance to the creature's movements, as, when walking slowly, it exhibits the creeping motion of a large reptile. The soft fur upon the hump and shoulders is manufactured by the natives of Tibet into a fine but strong cloth, and if submitted to the test of European skill, might no doubt be made to produce a very superior fabric. This animal is not generally fierce, but if intruded upon by strangers, it sometimes manifests very formidable symptoms of impatience. It has generally a sullen appearance, though that, I think, is greatly caused by the projecting forehead, which tends to give a stern aspect to the countenance. It, however, certainly expresses no signs of gratification when approached by those with whom it is most familiar, discovering none of those indications of pleasure so generally evinced by other animals under similar circumstances. When excited it is not easily appeased, and is exceedingly tenacious of injury, always showing great fierceness whenever any one approaches who has chanced to provoke it. The cow is called dhe, of which the wandering Tartars have large numbers. These Tartars, like the modern Bedouins and those nomadic races of more primitive times which nearly overspread the East, dwell chiefly under tents in the hills or in the deserts, wander from place to place, and have no means of subsistence but those supplied by their flocks and herds.

The yak, which they pasture upon the tops of the mountains and in the deep glens of Tibet, affords them at once warm clothing and wholesome food. They use it also as a beast of burden, and it answers the purpose of the horse in transporting them over those bleak and rugged mountains among which they dwell, as it is very strong and sure-footed. It scarcely ever falls, and when this does happen on steep declivities where it is so generally employed, the accident is almost invariably fatal. Instances of such casualties, however, are rare.

The herdsmen commonly convert the hides into a loose outer garment that covers the whole of their bodies, hanging down to the knees, and it proves a sufficient protection against the lowest temperature of the cold and desolate region which they inhabit. It furnishes at once a cloak by day and a bed by night. The long hair, when carefully taken from the skin, is skilfully manufactured into a sort of tent cloth which is remarkably strong and quite impervious to the wet. They convert the same material into ropes, which are much stronger than those composed of hemp and resist more successfully the influence of climate and of friction. The yak's tail is an indispensable appendage to the costume of an Eastern court; it is used throughout India, and when not to be obtained in sufficient quantities to answer the demand, is very successfully imitated by those cunning artificers, who are equalled only by the Chinese in these and similar deceptions. The tails are converted into chowries, a sort of whisk employed to keep off the flies and musquitoes from the heads of those who can afford such a luxury. The dhe, or cow of the yak, yields a large quantity of milk, and this is so rich as to produce better butter than that of any other of the bovine species in Asia.

We were much gratified at having the opportunity

of beholding so fine a creature of its kind, as this animal is seldom seen below the mountains of Tibet; no one, I believe, having yet thought it worth while to introduce the breed into Bengal, and most probably the experiment would fail if attempted.

CHAPTER III.

THE GHOORKAS.—COLONEL GILLESPIE.—SIEGE OF KALUNGA.

The independence of the Himalaya highlanders has been considerably shaken by the tyranny of the Ghoorkas, who, until dispossessed by the British government in India, during the Nepaul war, had entire possession of the southern side of these hills. The political condition of those mountaineers, being one of complete feudality, exhibited that want of general unity so prevalent in the feudal system, and which has always been the cause of much political mischief wherever it has prevailed. The whole district, which is of great extent, was divided into numerous petty states, each governed by an independent chief, and, as many of these rulers were little better than semi-barbarians, plunder was with them an honourable acquisition. Thus they were continually levying contributions on each other, the weakest upon the strongest, and were consequently involved in perpetual hostility.

In this condition of things, when the whole social system among them was in a perpetual state of jarring oscillation, accelerated by the stern and uncultured habits of the people, they were in a position to receive any ruler who should have the boldness to scale their mountain fastnesses and dictate laws to a community ready to obey any new master who should unite them under a less resolute but more prosperous domination.

The Ghoorka state, lying to the westward of Nepaul, was many years ago governed by an enterprising chieftain, who, determining upon the conquest of the hill country, directed all his faculties and means to this one object. He first subdued the fertile valley of Nepaul, which was the key to his further conquests. This valley contained a large extent of rich but unappropriated land, and promised, in the various productions of its soil, an abundant harvest to the conqueror. Upon the death of this chieftain, which happened not long after he had secured this important conquest, he was succeeded by his son, a stern yet enterprising warrior, who, pursuing his father's intention with that vigour so natural to his character and having now acquired a vast succession of means, turned his arms against the petty sovereigns of the hills, whom, after a short but spirited resistance, he completely subdued. He was finally assassinated and succeeded by an alien from his kindred, Ummur Sing Thappa, who usurped the sovereignty both of the Ghoorka state and of the mountainous districts on that side. It was under the rigid yoke of this tyrant that the hill-men suffered such a severe deprivation of liberty and independence.

The Ghoorka soldiers, severely but ably disciplined under experienced and sagacious leaders, are inferior to none and superior to most of the Indian troops who are unacquainted with the greater advantages of European tactics. They exhibit a perfect heedlessness of danger, and a readiness to meet any foe who may seek to be opposed to them. They consider obedience the first duty of a soldier, and freely sacrifice their lives in discharge of their military obligations, an infraction of which they look upon as the highest degradation. With no very accurate perception of moral right, and yet with a very high sense of moral obligation, they obey the dominant power by whom their allegiance is demanded with an undeviating and patient fidelity which in general nothing, not even the harshest treatment, can subdue. They have a high sense of honour, seldom betraying the trust reposed in them even by a stranger; while their long career of victory and their known determination in maintaining their conquests, rendered them no mean opponents to our armies during the Nepaul war.

As a proof of the resolute spirit by which the Ghoorka soldiers are actuated when engaged in defence of their conquests, I need only mention a memorable instance that occurred in the year 1814. A strong detachment, under the command of Colonel Gillespie, one of the most spirited officers in the British service, had been sent to besiege Kalunga, a small hill-fort in the Dhoon, and during the storming of which Colonel Gillespie was unhappily killed. The garrison consisted of about three hundred men, while the besiegers amounted to nearly three thousand, commanded by brave and experienced officers. After a desperate struggle, and with immense loss on the side of the besiegers, the fort was abandoned by the survivors among the besieged, amounting to seventy men out of three hundred, who, fighting their way through different passes which had been strongly guarded to cut off their retreat, eventually effected their escape with the loss of very few lives. Before daylight the officer who succeeded Colonel Gillespie in the command entered the fort, of which he took possession, though he found nothing but shattered walls and blackened ruins covered with the dead and dying. Here indeed was frightfully exhibited the desperate resistance which had been made by a few determined and but half-civilized soldiers against an immensely disproportioned force, highly disciplined and commanded by the ablest officers then under the British government in the East. What the besieged had done and suffered was incredible: they had displayed the highest endurance and the most indomitable courage. This was horribly apparent to the victors: their ears were shocked by the dismal groans of the dying, and their hearts saddened at the sight of mangled limbs which had been torn from their parent trunks by the bursting of the shells thrown into the fort from the besiegers' guns, and of disfigured bodies lying black and putrid on the very spot where they had fallen when struck down by the shot, which was scattered like hail over their weak defences, causing a most frightful carnage. The corpses of those who had perished early in the siege and had been just put under the surface of the ground, were seen protruding through the earth from their superficial graves in a revolting state of decay, exhaling the most noxious odours and filling the air with the seeds of pestilence. The bodies of women and children were among the dead and dying, some frightfully mangled but yet alive, and imploring most piteously for a drop of water to slake the raging thirst that was consuming them and adding an intolerable torment to their expiring agonies.

All that humanity could suggest was done for these unhappy sufferers, but so furious and deadly had been the cannonading before the fort surrendered, that few of the wounded survived. Upwards of a hundred dead bodies were committed to the pile by our native troops, and all the wounded put under the care of the surgeon who accompanied the British forces, by whose combined skill and attention several recovered, though most of them died. There were but few prisoners taken, and these were treated with great kindness, as a mark of their captors' respect for the bravery they had displayed in defence of Kalunga, which has seldom been equalled and never excelled in the annals of Indian warfare. It may stand a fair comparison with that so eminently signalised at the memorable siege of Bhurtpore, where the veteran Lake received the severest check experienced by him during his military career in the East, where he won immortal renown.

On this occasion, though the Ghoorkas had met with such severe losses, for they were defeated in almost every quarter by the superior discipline of our troops, still they manifested none of those symptoms of vindictive hostility which they have been represented as evincing in an earlier age, and which is common to many of the Indian races even at this day.

They made no unjust reprisals; they treated their prisoners with extreme humanity, expressing everywhere the greatest confidence in the British officers, whose superior tactics they extolled with the noble ingenuousness of a brave and generous enemy. One instance of this confidence deserves mention. While the cannonading was pouring death and devastation into the fort at every discharge, a wounded soldier of the enemy advanced to the breach and waved his hand as a signal for a parley. The firing immediately slackened and he came within our lines, where he was received with the greatest kindness. The lower part of his face had been dreadfully injured by a cannon-shot. He was immediately committed to the surgeon's care and eventually recovered, though after a long and dangerous confinement. When perfectly restored — in fact, as soon as he could safely travel — he returned to his party with an exalted feeling of patriotism which would have done honour to the worthiest cause, to assist, as he said, the struggles of his countrymen against their generous but national enemies. These struggles lasted not long and the mountaineers were soon released from the Ghoorka tyranny.

The natives of this wild and inhospitable country are in general not calculated to beget much sympathy either by their habits or appearance. In some districts there are, it is true, shades of difference, and occasionally there will be found a fine specimen of the hardy and generous mountaineer; but these instances are certainly not common. The men are for the most part of small stature, though their limbs are singularly muscular and elastic, betokening at once great strength and activity. Their countenances are not prepossessing; and whilst their whole aspect excites rather a feeling of compassion for their civil and social degradation, they confirm this unpleasant impression by the mean servility of their address. Even the higher classes of the peasantry, here called zemeendars, who have extensive farms and contrive to live in a state of great comparative comfort, are scarcely better conditioned in a moral point of view than the lowest of their dependants. They have the same vices of meanness, servility, and falsehood; they lie, cheat, and rob, where they have the opportunity, as if to lie, cheat, and rob were the three cardinal virtues. Their ignorance often shames humanity, and yet they possess in an eminent degree that well-disguised cunning so common to the most degraded intellects. They seek not to obtain knowledge, for they have no sympathy with it; to them it would be an unprofitable acquisition, a burden, from which release is therefore a joy. Even the highest orders, their princes, possess the elements of all these infirmities so conspicuous in the lower, and in proportion to their power are these vile propensities the cause of more or less mischief. They have no dignity of character, being utterly without honour or principle.

I have mentioned the extreme muscularity of limb possessed by these diminutive mountaineers, especially the poorer among them; indeed, their legs are generally disproportioned to their bodies, developing from the ankle to the hip a compages of muscles that would well become the members of a man six feet high, while their stature frequently does not exceed five. The hardy habits of these people will readily account for the extraordinary strength and size which their limbs attain. Accustomed to toil from their infancy up the mountain-steeps, and often with immense burdens, their muscles acquire an elasticity and power unknown in more level regions; while the excessive cold to which they are so often exposed braces and gives a tension to their fibres that enables them to endure almost any severity of climate. A hill-man will frequently carry a load of from ninety to a hundred pounds weight to a distance of eighteen miles over the most rugged paths where there appears scarcely footing for a goat: he will scale the almost perpendicular sides of hills and descend the most dangerous steeps without apprehension and apparently without difficulty. His dexterity is no less surprising than his strength, and the occurrence of any serious accident never appears to be contemplated. It is admirable to observe how the " human form divine" is adapted to master the difficulties of situation and climate; neither the asperities of the one nor the noxious influence of the other prevent him from finding a home with which he is content and in which he may be happy. Locality has, it is true, a great influence upon his moral and social condition; he is nevertheless everywhere the only creature that can surmount natural difficulties and render this world, under its most repulsive aspect, subservient to his wants: he is the creature of all climates, of all regions and equally wonderful in all.

The Himalaya mountaineers, in spite of their social degradation, are nevertheless in many respects an extraordinary race. The moral elements, indeed, exist among them, but these have not yet been excited into active and vigorous combination, for their vices prevail so completely over their brighter qualities, that the latter only occasionally scintillate through an intellectual darkness which is all but complete. The hill-man of this region is a slave to his passions and to his selfishness, the latter of which is so indelible within him that nothing can dislodge it. He is soon roused to anger and is then treacherous and cruel. He seldom fails to commit the most brutal excesses where the means are within his reach. He will rob whenever he has the opportunity, and impunity is his encouragement. He is not only violent and hasty, but also crafty and revengeful, and so profound is his duplicity, that he will frequently fawn at your feet with the most cringing humility while he holds the concealed dagger to plunge into your heart. The worst features of the Asiatic character are seen with most repelling prominence among the inhabitants of these mountains, originally imbibed, perhaps, in their occasional intercourse with the plains, and distorted into the wildest extremes by that impunity which is the curse of humanity and the privilege only of savages. Their princes offer them but a bad example by entertaining among themselves the deadliest animosities and displaying all the ferocious features so prominent in the feudal system in Europe during the middle ages. They acknowledge no law but the sword, no virtue but retaliation, no honour but revenge. So implacable sometimes are the feuds, even between the families of less distinguished note among them, that they are quenched only by the extermination of one or the other; while individual cases of revenge are scarcely less frequent and, perhaps, no less sanguinary than are to be found among the more brutalized population of central Africa. They who, from their superior birth and wealth, can command the devotion of their retainers by paying them the wages of plunder, attack and pillage their weaker neighbours, leaving them to their retaliation when they shall have acquired the means. They are almost invariably cruel and tyrannical masters, but to their superiors in power fawning and meanly subservient.

"The inhabitants of Nawar and Teekur," says Mr. Fraser, "are notorious for infamy of character even in this country, where all are bad. They are revengeful and treacherous, deficient in all good qualities, abandoned in morals and vicious in their habits. As a proof of the savage indifference with which they look on the life of another and on the act of shedding human blood, it is said that mere wantonness or a joke will induce the crime of putting a fellow-creature to death, merely for the satisfaction of seeing the blood flow and of marking the last struggles of their victim. Female chastity is here quite unknown, and murder, robbery, and outrage of every kind are regarded with indifference. They are generally unpleasing in appearance, mean, grovelling, cowardly, and cruel. It would seem as if the faint approaches they have made towards civilization, had only awakened the evil passions and propensities of the mind, which yet remains quite uncontrolled by, and ignorant of the restraint of religion and virtue. They have lost whatever native virtue may have existed in the savage state, and have not acquired that which would probably result from a happy, free and liberal intercourse with civilized beings."

The sillenies, or porters, a numerous class among the poorer population of these mountains, are so lazy as to require to be frequently urged forward by the rod, for they are deaf to persuasion. So great is their apathy, that they will often lay down their burdens in the most rugged passes and extend themselves upon the edge of a precipice where the slightest change of position would be inevitable destruction; and they submit to the severest castigation before their apathy is overcome or their latent passions can be roused. There are, it must be confessed, numerous exceptions, and these dark traits are perhaps to be accounted for by the tyranny to which they have so long been subservient, their excessive poverty and the barbarous ignorance in which they are suffered to live.

The Himalaya women are generally well favoured. They are neither so short of stature, nor so mean of aspect as the men. Their figures are finely proportioned, while their features possess that delicacy of proportion and softness of texture so peculiar to Hindoo females in their youth. They are much fairer than the women of the plains, being seldom darker than a native of Italy or Spain. They, however, soon lose their beauty, growing almost hideous in age. This loss—always a natural source of regret to the gentler sex in every country—is perhaps accelerated by constant exposure to the climate they live in, which is remarkable for very sudden and severe changes of temperature. Here they are not secluded as among the higher castes of Hindostan, and that fierce jealousy which is a dominant feeling of the Hindoo is entirely unknown in these hills, where the women enjoy a liberty as morally pernicious as it is socially degrading and of which they avail themselves to the fullest extent. They mix with the men without the slightest reservation, and this unlimited freedom of intercourse gives them a confidence and self-possession before strangers peculiar only to the highest classes of their sex in the most civilized countries.

The wives and daughters of these highlanders are their most valuable property: they labour in the farms with the ardour and address of men, and are thus wholly free from the slavish seclusion to which Hindoo and Mahomedan women are usually subjected. Their moral relaxation, however, subjects them to an evil worse than bondage. They soon exchange the delicate feelings of their sex for those which reduce them from all that is lovely in woman, to all that is debased. Chastity with them has neither

"A local habitation nor a name."

They are, however, neither beloved nor honoured by the men, who, though they set no value upon chastity, cannot regard those who uniformly violate it. Thus, though they do not check the sensuality of their females, they nevertheless do not respect it. The permission to do wrong does not always imply approbation, since a man, whose code of morals is loose or limited, may permit what he does not commend. The fact is, their apathy renders them insensible to those active jealousies which rage among the fiery temperaments that are warmed by a more glowing sun and fanned by more genial breezes. They therefore look without emotion upon what they probably neither honour nor approve. This indifference on one side and utter absence of chastity on the other, are supposed to be the proximate cause of one of the most singular and revolting customs to be found in the history of man; but I should rather consider them as the effect. These highlanders have almost in every district of this vast range of mountains a community of wives. The women are in fact polyandrists, as the Mahomedans are polygamists. One wife is often the common property of several brothers who are each legally bound to her by an indissoluble civil contract. They live in perfect harmony together, and it is surprising how rarely any difference occurs; for notwithstanding this debasing communion, they are governed by social laws to which they adhere with a scrupulous exactness utterly irreconcilable to such lax morality. The first child becomes the property of the elder husband, and so in rotation.

The general notions of these people regarding female virtue may be inferred from their admission of a practice so degrading to humanity, but its origin is perhaps to be looked for in causes remote and not immediately apparent. The practice of female infanticide among the Rajpoot tribes must have necessitated the search after wives from among those races claiming the nearest kindred with themselves, where they might be the most readily found. As the Himalaya mountaineers, on the southern side, claim an affinity with the Rajpoots, the draughts of women from the former to supply those which have been immolated in obedience to the barbarous prejudices of a proud but noble race, whose customs, however sanguinary, are inviolable laws to them, may account for that paucity of females in the mountains which renders polyandry a necessary evil. Certain it is, that the daughters of these highlanders are frequently taken to the plains and disposed of for prices according as the promise of beauty is greater or otherwise; so that the deficiency caused by this singular trait of sordidness and parental indifference, may account for a practice which however revolting to our better feelings, becomes a matter of civil expediency. The Rajpoot immolations* must reduce that tribe to the necessity of seeking for wives somewhere; and if it be a matter of uncertainty whence they obtain them, the existence of polyandry among the inhabitants of the Himalaya mountains appears to me at once to solve the problem.

* Until within the last thirty years, it was a practice among the Rajpoot tribes to destroy their female children as soon as they were born, lest their parents should not be able to find them suitable alliances. This horrible custom was suppressed through the instrumentality of Mr. Duncan, formerly Governor of Bombay, and, I believe, no longer exists.

CHAPTER IV.

HOUSES OF THE HILL-MEN.—CIVILIAN IN CALCUTTA.

It is remarkable that a race so degraded in morals as the Himalaya mountaineers, and whose general habits are so remote from those of a civilized people, should occasionally assume an external refinement, to which nations standing much higher in the scale of positive civilization, are comparatively strangers. Notwithstanding their brutal habits in other respects and the cringing servility with which they approach a superior, or any one who has the means of benefiting them, they have, nevertheless, an ease and amenity of manner not at all inferior to the highlanders of European countries. Their address is commonly free and unembarrassed, except when they have any ulterior object in view, in which case they exhibit all the mean humiliation of semi-barbarians. They are for the most part comfortably clad and their houses well constructed, clean and convenient, by comparison with those of the poor who inhabit the Alps or the highlands of Scotland. The very lowest among them are indeed an exception, for poverty and destitution are peculiar to no country but known in all.

The farmers of these mountains display no little skill in agriculture when the stubborn nature of the ground which they have to till and the natural difficulties of situation are considered. It is surprising to see the steep sides of hills, so rugged and precipitous that you would scarcely suppose they could be adventured on by the foot of man, covered with the ripening harvest, the fruits at once of his agricultural skill and of his laborious industry. The rough rocks and shaggy steeps are converted into fruitful fields; " the pastures are covered with flocks, the valleys also are covered with corn ;" and it is one of the most gratifying sources of reflection, in a region where the natural and moral features are generally so repulsive, to find that man, even in his lowest state of social degradation, has still something to exalt him in human estimation.

The houses of the hill-men are upon the whole tolerably convenient, and with reference to the general habits of their occupants, sufficiently clean. They consist of two or more stories, the lower appropriated to lumber and stabling for their cattle, the higher to the dwelling of the family. The rooms are floored with planks, I think of pine, well fitted and planed; they are not large, but very conveniently disposed so as to admit light to the best advantage and exclude cold. The windows, which are merely small apertures in the wall, always open on the sheltered side of the house, and the builders never introduce more than absolutely necessary. In order to shut out the cold, as their windows are not glazed and they have no substitute for glass, they cover them at night with a piece of thin board very accurately fitted, which answers the purpose exceedingly well. The walls of their houses are plastered with mud, upon which are frequently painted some of the strange figures represented in their barbarous mythology. The fireplace is always in the centre of the room and consists merely of a stone hearth upon which the fire is kindled, and as there is no chimney, the smoke finds egress through the windows; but as these are extremely small the sooty exhalation becomes intolerable, except to those familiarized to it by long habit. The family all sleep together on one bed, which consists of a layer of soft grass spread in a corner of the room under the windows, so as to be sheltered from the night-air which cannot be entirely excluded. The only furniture in these houses is a few earthen vessels of various sorts and for different purposes. The ascent to each story is by a thick pole notched at intervals of about a foot, which the inmates ascend with quickness and dexterity.

Although tolerably clean, it is impossible to exclude from these mountain-abodes the vermin that abound in this region to such a degree as to prove an intolerable nuisance to strangers. The natives, however, seem to consider this visitation rather an advantage than a nuisance, as the insects continually swarming over their bodies excite an irritation on the skin which prevents the superficial circulation from languishing and thus leaving that torpor so common in a cold climate, unless the circulation be kept in constant activity. When their bodies are so covered that the accession becomes troublesome, they plunge into water with their clothes on, thus destroying in a few moments myriads of these importunate visitants.

The contrast between the mansion of an aristocratic civilian in Calcutta and the rude cottages of these hardy mountaineers is sufficiently striking. The former has everything around him which wealth can procure. Seated on an easy chair of the coolest construction, one leg carelessly thrown upon a handsome mahogany table, the other languidly resting on a costly morah,* he smokes his hookah in all the indolent luxury of a temperature of ninety-four degrees. His sircar† advances with a profound salaam to receive his orders for the day; the hookahbadar‡ stands ready to replace the exhausted chillum, the peadah§ to bear his master's commands wherever he may choose to have them conveyed, and the punka-bearer to fan him with the broad leaf of the palmyra. Every want is anticipated: all he has to do for himself is to think, and as soon as his wishes are expressed they are executed. His hair is dressed, his beard shaved, his feet are washed, and his nails pared, by his ready attendants. When he lolls on his couch, he is fanned by an obedient Mussulman or Hindoo; when he sleeps, a yak's tail is waved over his head in gentle and cooling undulations to keep off the obtrusive musquitoes, which would otherwise "mark him for their own;" when he retires to his nightly repose, he is undressed by his obsequious valet, and when he rises from his luxurious slumbers he is

* Footstool.
† The sircar is a sort of house-steward.
‡ The hookahbadar always stands behind the hookah, so that he does not appear in the engraving.
§ The peadah is a running-footman.

dressed by the same hand. When he goes abroad he is borne on the shoulders of four sturdy retainers and attended by as many more; or, when he chooses to go on foot—covered by a chatta,* which glitters with its costly array in the sunbeams, and followed by a host of servitors of various ranks and designations—his walk for pleasure or for exercise is a positive procession.

To the Himalaya hill-men such luxuries are unknown; they, however, in their wild but picturesque abodes, perched upon the crest of a mountain hanging over the roaring torrent and deriding, as it were, the earthquake and the storm, are far higher objects of human sympathy than the mere sybarite, who is rather the victim of civilization than a living evidence of its triumph. In these mountains a solitary dwelling is seldom seen; the houses are clustered together in tens and twenties upon the faces of the hills, dotting their dark shaggy sides and forming compact villages which impart an agreeable variety to the prospect. Every village has its temple, which is always a rude structure, though devoid neither of elegance nor of just architectural proportions. These humble sanctuaries sometimes tower to the height of from sixty to seventy feet, and are divided into several stories. The means of ascending from one story to the other are the same as in the houses, by a pole deeply notched, which serves as a ladder. The religion of these children of the hills seems to be a blending of that of all the different Hindoo sects, while their priests appear no better instructed in

* An umbrella.

the Shasters, Vedahs and Puranas,* than themselves.

In some districts of these mountains they have a most singular mode of sepulture. When a person dies and leaves behind him the means of paying for an expensive funeral, it is the practice to treat his corpse in a manner which most wealthy persons, I should imagine, would rather shrink from with horror than anticipate with satisfaction. They first carefully wash the body, and after having prepared it for the principal process with a variety of ceremonies, they cast it into a huge mortar, where they reduce it, bones and all, to a thick pulp, which is rolled up into small balls; these are taken to a spot consecrated for this particular purpose, and strewed upon the ground, when they are instantly devoured by kites which always hover about these places of interment in great numbers. Those kites are considered sacred by the priests, who regularly feed them, as to those holy men they are a source of no small emolument. There are certain persons appointed to watch these birds, lest they should be driven from their favourite haunts, or otherwise molested. No one but their accredited guardians are permitted to approach them, though this precaution scarcely seems necessary, for the superstition of the populace is so great, that they would consider it an act of the most flagrant impiety to intrude upon the retreat of those feathered anthropophagi. To be "emboweled" in the maws of the sacred kites is a very expensive mode of sepulture, and is entirely

* The sacred books of the Hindoos.

confined to the higher classes. The poor are buried in various ways: sometimes they are burned, sometimes cast into the nearest river, and they are not unfrequently left upon the peak of some solitary mountain to be devoured by the vultures.

In certain districts the inhabitants expose the bodies of their friends and relations in a similar manner to be eaten by carnivorous creatures, with only this difference, that the corpses are laid out with great ceremony within a walled area, being placed upon iron gratings over a deep vault and left uncovered, in order that they may be the more readily devoured. A similar practice prevails among the Parsees at Bombay, who are a remnant of the Guebres, or ancient fire-worshippers. In order to exclude the horrible sight of the carnival within, those cemeteries are surrounded by a lofty wall, in which there is a large aperture to admit dogs, jackals, and other beasts of prey, that crowd daily in great numbers to these disgusting receptacles for the dead.

The animals found in the Himalaya mountains are neither so numerous nor so fierce as those on the plains. In the lower regions of the hills the elephant is sufficiently common and the rhinoceros is sometimes seen, though not frequently. Tigers and leopards inhabit the forests but rarely frequent the higher situations. There are deer of various sorts and very numerous. Wild hogs are by no means rare, though neither so large nor so fierce as in the level country. Buffaloes are also indigenous to this sequestered region, but they confine themselves to the bases of the mountains. Hares, monkeys, jackals, foxes, likewise find a refuge in these hilly solitudes.

> "Fierce o'er the mountain stalks the ravenous tiger,
> Or lurks in gloomy caves; through the thick grass
> Coils the vast serpent, on whose painted back
> The cricket chirps, and with the drops that dew
> The scales, allays his thirst. Silence profound
> Enwraps the forest, save where babbling springs
> Gush from the rock, or where the echoing hills
> Give back the tiger's roar, or where the boughs
> Burst into crackling flame, and wide extends
> The blaze the dragon's fiery breath has kindled."*

The trees in these regions are sometimes of enormous size, occasionally measuring twenty feet in girth, towering to a height of more than a hundred and fifty, and exhibiting a sheer branchless trunk at least sixty feet high, surmounted by a vast crest which waves like a gigantic canopy above it, projecting its mighty shadow in the calm clear light of the setting sun and wrapping in solemn shade the scarped and precipitous sides of the neighbouring hill. Everything here is, in fact, on so immense a scale, that all minuter objects are lessened to a degree hardly to be conceived. At a short distance, a man seems dwindled to a mere puppet, while horses and oxen appear scarcely bigger than dogs.

The most singular animal known in these hills is the musk-deer, a creature timid and wild to excess; it lives secluded from the sight of man, and indeed of every other animal but its own species, inhabiting the

---

* "Specimens of the Hindoo Theatre," translated from the original Sanscrit by Horace Hayman Wilson, Esq., Professor of Sanscrit at the University of Oxford.

most inaccessible heights and living among glens and precipices that defy the approach of human foot, in a neighbourhood where the cold is intense and the snows are eternal. It is seldom seen at an altitude lower than twelve thousand feet above the sea, though sometimes forced to quit the heights in search of pasture, which is scanty in proportion as the snowy regions are approached.

The musk-deer, when full grown, is about the size of a calf six months old; it is singularly shaped, having a head which much resembles that of a wild hog, while its feet are precisely those of a deer. The snout is sharp and the countenance wrinkled; the eye small, dark, bright, and full. From the upper jaw two long tusks project, pointing downwards in a gentle curve and extending several inches beyond the lower mandible. This animal is extremely active, and so shy that it is difficult to be met with, and no less difficult to be secured when killed; for its general haunts are so sequestered and often in such inaccessible places, that if shot, even the hill-men sometimes dare not venture to approach their quarry. The musk is contained in a small bag under the belly and this bag is cut from the creature alive; for it is said that, should the animal be killed before the bag can be disengaged from its body, the musk is almost instantly taken up by the absorbents, which so taints the flesh that it is rendered unfit for human food. The musk-deer is so scarce that, whenever one is seen, the whole population of the district quit their homes to join in the chase and it is at least an equal chance whether the anxious object of pursuit is taken or escapes.

The musk of this animal is very expensive and difficult to be procured in its genuine state, as the natives manufacture a counterfeit article, which is exported in immense quantities to China, through Tibet, and to the plains of Hindostan.

There are several birds peculiar to these mountains, and among the most remarkable is the rutnal. It is very large and more beautiful than the pheasant, of which it is a species; it exceeds the latter in size and is less delicately shaped, though greatly surpassing it in splendour of plumage. The body is entirely of a deep brilliant blue, without the slightest variation of tint; while the neck is of an intense purple so richly blended with green and scarlet as to glisten in the sun's rays, and throwing off a continued succession of scintillations which sparkle like a glory round it. The back, when uncovered by the wings, is white: and as soon as the bird takes flight it spreads out a copious tail, the feathers of which are a bright cinnamon-colour. There is a large tuft on the head, beautifully variegated, which it can erect or depress at will, forming a graceful crest and adding greatly to the splendour of the neck and breast. At the moment of taking wing the rutnal gives a soft, clear whistle which is heard at a considerable distance. This bird is exceedingly wild and therefore not frequently met with; like the musk-deer, it lurks in the highest recesses of the mountains, seeking the most sequestered spots and delighting in the dreariest solitudes, where human foot seldom dares to penetrate. From this cause it is rarely to be obtained. Its flesh is said to be delicate above that of every other game bird, though many of the natives who have passed a tolerably long life in the vicinity of its haunts have never enjoyed the luxury of tasting it. There are several birds of the pheasant species in these lofty districts, but none so beautiful in plumage or so much esteemed for the table.

Another bird is found here, less difficult of approach, but, perhaps partly for this reason, much less highly esteemed. The cock-bird is as large as a common dunghill-fowl, with a clear brown plumage and a small delicate head something resembling that of the rock-pigeon. It is by no means scarce, but in every respect inferior to the pheasant.

The hill-partridge abounds in the mountain-forests, and I know of no game so exquisite in flavour. It is moreover a very graceful bird, having a much more delicate form than the common partridge and bearing a nearer resemblance to the quail, which, however, it far exceeds in richness of plumage: this is greatly varied, though red and black prevail. It has a singular habit of basking in the sun covered with dust, appearing like a dry molehill until disturbed, when it rises with a sudden bound, shakes off the dust, expands its beautiful wings in the sunbeams, as if conscious of the splendour in which nature had arrayed it, and disappears in the impenetrable recesses of the forests.

The black partridge so general throughout India is equally plentiful in these hills: the flesh of this bird is likewise very delicate and the plumage far superior to that of the common partridge of Europe. The jungle-fowl, of which I have before spoken, are also numerous, though so wild that they are not easy to be approached. They seldom fly, but run into the thickest parts of the jungles where it is impossible to follow them. The only way to obtain a shot at them is to watch just after daybreak at the edge of the forests, from which they come in great numbers to feed; they are then easily killed. Like most of the game birds in these high regions, their plumage is richly varied and their flesh delicately flavoured.

In our progress from the plains to Serinagur we were much struck with the simple manner in which the mountaineers manage their bees, and of these they generally possess numerous swarms. They devote great attention to them, repaying the labours of these industrious insects with great kindness and care. In this respect, if in no other, our rustics might learn from them a valuable lesson. As honey forms a favourite article of food among the Himalaya highlanders, they have a very extensive sale for it; it is therefore with them a great article of internal commerce, in fact, the staple of their bazaars, where it always finds a ready vent. They obtain the honey without destroying the bees by means of a hollow cylinder of wood inclosed in the wall of their huts on the side most sheltered from the weather, and in which there is an opening without for the bees to enter. In the centre of this hive there is a moveable division which is kept open while the bees are making their honey; but, as soon as the combs are full, the busy family is driven out by a noise made through the inward extremity. As soon as they have retreated, the central partition is closed and the combs are drawn out of the cylinder from the opening on the inner wall. The honey being secured, the hive is again opened and the bees commence their interminable labour of reproduction.

Serinagur, where we halted, is the capital of Gurwhal and situated on the south bank of the Alacananda river, which is the main stream of the sacred Ganges, about seven leagues above its junction with the Bhageruttee, where a belt of level ground extends to a distance of several miles, forming the beautiful valley of Serinagur. This city was once a place of considerable importance and a mart for the productions of the countries on either side of the Snowy Mountains. It was dreadfully shattered by an earthquake in the year 1803. Since that time it has been in a state of comparative decay, and will most probably never be restored.

CHAPTER V.

NUJIBABAD.—NUJIB UD DOWLAH'S TOMB.

After remaining a few days at Serinagur, where we were treated with great kindness by the Rajah, we set out on our return towards the plains. We reached Nujibabad in about four days, pitched our tents and made a short stay there. It is a small town built by Nujib ud Dowlah, a Rohilla chief of some note in his day, for the purpose of attracting the commerce between Cashmere and Hindostan. It is situated about twenty miles to the south-east of Hurdwar, and is ninety-five miles from Delhi. It was a place of some importance, though since the earthquake at Serinagur, which has interrupted the traffic extensively enjoyed by the latter town before that event, Nujibabad has been involved in the same commercial privation. Of late years its commerce has almost totally declined, a circumstance perhaps to be finally attributed to the severe shock which the Rohilla power received from the British arms during the Nepaul war. It is now inhabited by few persons of either wealth or consideration, and bids fair in another generation to be the abode only of " the moles and of the bats."

The town is about three-quarters of a mile in

length, and pleasantly situated on the northern bank of a small lake. The streets are in general broad, regular, and remarkably clean for an Indian town. They are divided by barriers at different intervals, forming distinct bazaars in which the scene is sufficiently busy, although much less variety is now displayed there than formerly. A traffic of great extent used to be carried on at Nujibabad in wood, bamboos, copper, tincal, musk, and honey, from the hills. In the height of its prosperity it was also the entrepôt of a trade from Lahore, Cashmere, and Cabul, to the east and south-east of Hindostan. The situation of the town is low and the surrounding country swampy; thus in consequence of the superabundant vegetation collecting and condensing the exhalations, together with the various vegetable substances continually scattered over the surface of the soil being put into a state of active fermentation by the heat reflected from the neighbouring hills, the atmosphere is very uncongenial to any but a native constitution. Even the natives themselves do not exhibit that bodily energy and muscular vigour of frame so common to the more hardy inhabitants of the mountains.

In the neighbourhood of Nujibabad are the remains of some fine buildings, and just without the town is seen the tomb of its founder, Nujib ud Dowlah. Though distinguished by little ornament, it is nevertheless imposing from the quiet elegance and solemn simplicity of its structure. It is a square building flanked with four cupolas stuccoed with chunam, and having a dome covered with the same material rising out of the centre. It is protected by four massy stone walls, forming a quadrangle, with strong square bastions at each angle; and there is a plain gateway in the centre of the front wall of the area which encloses the mausoleum. This monument stands upon the border of the lake, which when swelled by the rains, almost washes the lateral wall on the southern side, giving an agreeable relief to the wildness of the surrounding scene.

The view of the distant mountains from the plain on which this mausoleum stands, is grand in the extreme. The snowy range is distinctly visible and its white peaks lifting their spotless crests above the clouds and appearing to shoot up into the very skies as if they had set at defiance the elementary law of limitation, produce a truly sublime effect. Their gelid spires, capped with eternal snow, are strikingly imposing in the midst of their cold and repulsive solitude; for the eye as well as the mind can never be directed, without an impressive emotion, towards those regions of unvarying sterility and silence where human foot has never penetrated and no living creature has ever found a permanent abode. Such a scene baffles the force of words, nor can those impressions which are excited by the contemplation of nature in her most inspiring solemnities, be communicated by any written description.

The country at the base of the hills in this neighbourhood, is well cultivated and very fertile. The labours of the husbandman, which are light and quickly accomplished, are soon repaid by an abundant harvest. The eminences skirting the plain and forming the lower range of that chain of mountains

which divides Hindostan from Tibet and Tartary, are about eight leagues from the spot where we had now halted, although they did not appear above half a dozen miles. Such is their altitude and bulk that so short a distance scarcely seems to diminish them to the eye, which is, moreover, beguiled by the extreme clearness of the atmosphere.

Near Nujib ud Dowlah's tomb is a tope of stately trees that overshadows some fine ruins, several of which are on the skirts of the town. Behind these trees there is a mausoleum of considerable beauty, highly ornamented with mosaics of black and white marble; the chief object of interest, however, is the tomb of the founder of Nujibabad. Wild elephants and tigers abound in this neighbourhood, where the jungles are very extensive and in many places perfectly impenetrable. The clear, doleful wail of the jackal is heard at night, waking the mountain echoes which multiply the din, to the great annoyance of the weary traveller, though it seems to produce but little inconvenience to those whom habit has reconciled to so loud and dissonant a lullaby.

Before we quitted Nujibabad, we had the opportunity of seeing a bull-fight, an amusement not unfrequently indulged in by the petty Rajahs of the mountain districts. These bulls had been brought from Boutan, and were exhibited by a party of jugglers, who expected a small gratuity from each spectator. The animals were about the size of a Bengal ox, or of an English bull two years and a half old. They had, however, no excrescence between the shoulders, common to the Bengal breed, and, unlike that species generally, were sleek, fat, and extremely fierce. They had little sharp horns, which were very smooth and bore a fine polish. Their fore legs were so short that but for the prodigious depth from the upper part of the shoulder to the extremity of the neck, they would have appeared stunted and disproportioned. From the extreme narrowness of the loins, compared with the depth and breadth of the fore-quarters, their hind legs seemed much too long. Their necks were very thick, indicating amazing strength, which they sufficiently manifested in the issue, while their heads were delicately small. They were of a deep liver colour. When brought into the area, being led by strong ropes attached to their horns and noses, they pawed the ground, threw themselves into the most violent contortions, and exhibited every symptom of the most desperate ferocity. The men who led them forward showed great dexterity in managing these impetuous animals, adroitly avoiding their plunges and bringing them to a degree of control quite surprising, considering the intense excitement under which they were evidently labouring.

The bulls seemed perfectly to comprehend why they were led into the area, betraying the most violent symptoms of impatience to try their prowess, while the spectators were no less impatient to witness a scene as novel as it promised to be terrific. At a given signal the ropes were slipped from the creatures' heads and they were left at liberty. In a moment they sprang forward as if to ascertain whether they were really released from the restraint of the ropes, then curving their backs, like a strung bow, as preparing to exert their utmost strength, they tore up the ground with their horns, plunged and roared, their eye-balls at the same time projecting from the sockets with a savage stare and flashing with the most portentous fury. They ran wildly round the area for more than a minute before they came in contact, gradually narrowing the circuit as if collecting themselves for the onslaught; each watching to take his adversary at an advantage. At length they met each other full in front, darted forward with astonishing celerity, and tremendous indeed was the shock! Both staggered for an instant but bore the concussion without giving way, when their horns became locked and then commenced the grand struggle for victory. Fierce as the onset had been, it did not appear in the slightest degree to have diminished the energies of these pugnacious animals. On the contrary, without wounding each other and their horns continuing locked, they displayed wonderful strength and dexterity, each preventing the other from goring him; so that the contest was really far less terrible than might have been anticipated from the manner in which they commenced the encounter. They were occupied full twenty minutes in this energetic struggle without disengaging their horns, exerting all the while their utmost strength to cast one another upon the ground. Alternately retreating and advancing, as their powers relaxed or recurred, the earth flew from their heels in showers while they pressed their hard heads together with still more determined obstinacy and with the might which rage added to their ordinary strength. At length the weaker began to retreat, and as he retreated, the other, feeling his advantage, pushed on with renewed vigour. He felt that he was about to conquer, and with a roar of anticipated triumph forced his adversary on his haunches. At this moment the keepers advanced, and by striking the victor on the nose with a large bamboo, forced him to disengage his horns, when they secured both the combatants with cords and led them from the area amid the cheers of the gratified spectators.

During our stay at Nujibabad the thermometer in our tents rose occasionally as high as a hundred and five degrees. Upon our departure from this town we proceeded to Kerutpoor, a distance of about twelve miles. We found the country in our route generally well cultivated. The view of the distant mountains was very striking, especially at sunrise, when their broad bosoms, catching the level rays, cast them with subdued splendour over the neighbouring plains.

At Chandpoor, our next halting-place, we received much attention from the chief of the district, to whom we had letters of introduction. He was unusually hospitable and strongly pressed us to extend our stay. He was fond of field sports, and before we quitted the neighbourhood, afforded us an opportunity of witnessing a somewhat novel mode of catching the tiger. It had been ascertained that one of those destructive animals was in a jungle at some short distance, and had taken up its abode within the cover of a thick brake at the very verge of the wood. It had been scared from its covert the preceding day, when a large hole about six feet square and twelve feet deep was dug within a dozen yards of its lair. The sides of the hole rather sloped inward from the top to the bottom so as to increase the difficulty of escape, of which indeed there was little chance, should the animal fall into the snare.

Early in the evening before the tiger returned, a goat was placed upon a small platform slightly fixed in the centre of the hole, on a level with the surrounding surface and supported by weak bamboos; so that little additional weight would precipitate it into the chasm below. The rest of the surface above was covered with grass, and no appearance of an opening remained. The night happened to be unusually dark and we repaired early in the morning to the spot where this preparation had been made for entrapping the sanguinary tyrant of the forest. When at some distance, perceiving that the bait had not been taken, we concealed ourselves behind a few intervening trees to see if the tiger would quit the place of his security and fall into the snare that had been so ingeniously placed to betray him. We had not waited above half an hour when our wishes were gratified by observing the beautiful beast rush from its lurking-place, and, when within about five yards of the devoted goat, spring upon it with a yell so ferocious that I trembled where I stood, though removed from all chance of danger. The platform instantly gave way with a crash, and the tiger and goat both fell into the hollow beneath. As soon as the former found itself a prisoner it howled with rage, lashed its sides with its tail, erected the fur upon its back and exhibited fearful demonstrations of fury. It made the most desperate efforts to escape, springing up the sides of the shaft and occasionally clinging to the very edge; the earth however was so soft that there was no hold for its claws, so that it always fell back; but upon reaching the ground and finding its efforts at release invariably foiled, its fury redoubled. Its yells were dreadful. The goat was quite dead but remained untouched by its destroyer, which at length lay upon its belly almost exhausted with its exertions. At this moment our host advanced and fired at the dreaded captive as it lay panting and powerless. The ball took effect but not mortally. The sudden pang only roused the tiger to renewed exertions in order to retaliate upon its assailant, who deliberately loaded and fired until the excited beast was destroyed. So tenacious was it of life, that it received seven balls in different parts of its body before it finally surrendered to the great conqueror—death.

Upon quitting Chandpore we passed through large tracts of jungle, in which peafowl greatly abounded. We forbore, however, from shooting any in deference to the prejudices of the people, who look upon the peacock as a consecrated bird. During the night the wind rose so high that our tents were in danger of being prostrated, and became so saturated with rain, which fell in torrents, as to be too heavy for the camels to carry; we were therefore obliged to keep them standing the best part of the succeeding day in order to get them dry.

On approaching the Ganges we found the country more open and agreeable. A few miles from Sumbul a large herd of deer crossed our route, one of which was shot by an armed attendant who had secreted himself behind a ruin; for these animals are so timid that it is very difficult to get near them.

At Sumbul there is a mosque of considerable beauty, though not much respected, built by the unfortunate but virtuous Humāyūn. The town is but thinly populated and many of the houses are altogether deserted. The bazaars being indifferently attended, there is little or no appearance of that busy chaffering so generally observed in the bazaar of an Indian town. We crossed the Ganges at the Depour Gaut, proceeded to Anopshur, a military station above Futtyghur, and after a progress of four days, crossed the Kyratta Gaut on the Jumna and entered the still splendid capital of the Mogul empire. But Delhi is no longer what it was during the domination of the house of Timour. Its glory has departed, though it is magnificent even in its decay.

The modern city of Delhi, and the seat of the present Mahomedan empire in Hindostan—alas, how fallen! was built by Shah Jehan in the seventeenth century and called after him Shahjehanabad. It is about seven miles in circumference and stands on the western bank of the Jumna. It is protected by a strong lofty wall, but which would offer little effectual resistance to modern artillery. There is nothing very remarkable in the town which yields in magnificence to many of inferior note in Hindostan. It has seven gates, near one of which is a college, a tolerably handsome edifice of some extent but now unappropriated and rapidly falling to decay. The palaces of Saadet Khan, and of Sultan Darah Shekoh are fine structures, standing within large enclosures and encompassed by lofty walls, within which are baths, menageries, stables, and various other subsidiary buildings. In this quarter of the city are several handsome mosques, and here is the celebrated Musjid, where, in 1739, the sanguinary Persian conqueror Nadir Shah sat and witnessed the massacre of the unfortunate inhabitants.

The gardens of Shalimar, made when the modern city was built, are said to have cost upwards of a hundred lacs of rupees, or above a million sterling. They were originally surrounded by a high brick wall, and occupied a space above a mile in circumference. They are now so completely in ruins that scarcely a vestige of their former magnificence remains. From the southern wall of these gardens, as far as the eye can reach, the champaign presents nothing but one vast surface covered with splendid ruins, the remnants of the former Indraprastha.* The whole plain is crowded with these magnificent remains. Mosques, mausoleums, palaces, observatories, pavilions, colleges, baths, seraglios, lie heaped in mighty confusion, showing, in the lapsing glories of their decay, what must have been the grandeur of that city which they contributed to adorn during the period of its strength and of its pride. Even Upper Egypt, so rich in memorials of former greatness, can exhibit nothing superior to the monumental relics that lie scattered over the plains on which ancient Delhi originally stood. But though this once magnificent capital has passed away and is now little more than a me-

---

* Indraprastha is the Sanscrit name of old Delhi.

morandum in the chronicle of time, other cities have sprung up by the application of human energies, if not equally magnificent, at least of equal importance. Nothing passes from us without a purpose. For every loss there is a balance of gain. One man dies and another is born. One empire is crushed and expires, when another starts into existence and flourishes If ruin lays her mighty grasp upon some distinguished capital, prosperity lifts another from the shade.

"The spider," says a Persian poet, "has wove its web in the palace of the emperors, and the owl hath sung her watch-song on the towers of Afrasiab."

<pre>
Look Nature through, 'tis revolution all—
All change, no death. Day follows night, and night
The dying day; stars rise and set, and rise;
Earth takes the example. See the Summer gay,
With her green chaplet and ambrosial flowers,
Droops into pallid Autumn: Winter gray,
Horrid with frost and turbulent with storms,
Blows Autumn, and his golden fruits, away,
Then melts into the Spring: soft Spring, with breath
Favonian, from warm chambers of the south
Recalls the first. All, to reflourish, fades:
As in a wheel, all sinks to reascend,
Emblem of man who passes, not expires.
</pre>

CHAPTER VI.

A GOSSEIN.—GHOLAUM KAUDIR.—THE SERAGLIO.

ONE morning, as I was about to quit my tent, which was pitched a short distance without the walls of Delhi in a fine tope of tamarind-trees, I perceived a gossein standing with his back against a broken pillar at a short distance from me. He had assumed that attitude which betokened an expectation of receiving something more tangible than mere courtesy from the benevolence of myself or any other person whom he might thus silently condescend to supplicate; for with these devotees the social order of things is frequently inverted: they consider the recipient the benefactor when of their own community, or the giver the beneficiary when of any other. As I came near him I perceived that he had a thick iron rod passed through his cheeks, riveted at each end, from which a circular piece of iron depended inclosing the chin. Though the rod passed quite through the tongue, as I afterwards found, it did not materially affect his articulation: he spoke with some difficulty but was nevertheless perfectly intelligible. He was an elderly man of gentle manners and mild aspect, without being offensively filthy, as the members of this strange tribe so frequently are. I invited him to enter the tent, which he immediately did, and to my surprise was very communicative. The iron through his tongue and cheeks had been a penitential infliction to which he had submitted in consequence of the breach of a vow. He declined my invitation to seat himself, but stood erect with his back against the pole of the tent and entered freely into conversation upon the strange events of his life, answering all my questions with the most perfect readiness, and he appeared gratified at giving me any information either respecting himself or the singular customs of the religious fraternity to which he belonged.

He stated that he was then under a vow to remain erect for the space of fifteen years. During thirteen of this term he had either stood or walked; yet he suffered little or no inconvenience, sleeping every night in the jungles with his back against a tree as soundly as the most voluptuous man could upon a bed of down. He confessed, however, that for some time after he had commenced the performance of this strange vow he was obliged to be supported with cords when inclined to sleep, and his feet swelled to such a painful degree that he could scarcely stand or walk. After a time, however, this inconvenience ceased, when the performance of his penance became no longer either a pain or a grief to him.

This was not the only infliction to which he had voluntarily subjected himself; the fingers of his left hand were so completely bent upward from the palm as to form a right angle with the back of the hand, and were thus rendered entirely useless. He further told me that he had been suspended from the branch of a tree during three hundred and sixty-five revolutions of the earth, as he expressed it, or a whole year. He was suspended by a cord with a strong bamboo crossing the end, upon which he sat, while a strap confined him to the rope and thus prevented his falling: this he described as the severest infliction to which he had ever submitted. I gave him a trifling gratuity with which he departed perfectly satisfied.

The self-tortures inflicted by these fanatics are entirely voluntary; they are, like many of the Roman Catholic penances, merely acts of supererogation and are not necessarily enjoined in the Hindoo ritual, as will appear from the Mahabbarat, a work esteemed almost of divine authority among the Hindoos.* " Those men who perform severe mortifications of the flesh not authorised by the Sastra are possessed of hypocrisy and pride; they are overwhelmed with lust, passion and tyrannic strength. Those fools torment the spirit that is in the body and myself who am in them." †

Whilst we remained at Delhi, I could not help contrasting the wretched condition of the reigning emperor with that of its former sovereigns, who established the Mogul dominion upon the ruins of the Afghan or Patan dynasty and erected the standard of the crescent in almost every district of Hindostan. The late emperor, Shah Allum the Second, exhibited

---

* See the Bhagvat Geeta, an episode of the Mahabbarat, translated by Sir Charles Wilkins from the original Sanscrit, lecture xvii. page 120.

† This is spoken by Krishna, the chief avatar or incarnation of Vishnu.

in his establishment the sad decline into which the Mahomedan sovereignty had fallen. In 1788, Gholaum Kaudir, a Rohilla chief, in whom the too confiding emperor had reposed implicit confidence, made a sudden irruption upon Delhi, of which he became master, seized the weak but virtuous Shah Allum and after subjecting him for several weeks to the most humiliating mortifications, loading him with insults and exposing him to every atrocious abuse in order to extort from him the supposed secret of his concealed treasures, pierced the unhappy emperor's eyes with his crease;* thus rendering him totally blind. He likewise massacred and put to the torture several members of the royal family; nor did he quit the city, where he had indeed rendered the imperial palace a house of mourning, until the approach of Mahadajee Scindia's army drove him from the scene of his atrocities. A retribution, however, as sudden as it was terrible shortly overtook him: he was pursued and captured by a detachment of the Mahratta army and brought before their commander. Scindia did not deign to utter a word, but, looking sternly on the hardened criminal, who seemed to despise the fate which he too well knew awaited him, ordered one of his attendants to ask him where he had deposited the plunder of the palace, and, on his refusing to answer, the Rohilla was given up to a truly terrible punishment: he was put into an iron cage and suspended from a beam in front of the army. After being exposed to the scoffs of men scarcely less ferocious than himself, his nose, ears, hands, and feet, were cut off, his eyes forced from

* A short two-edged dagger.

their sockets, and in this mutilated state he was ordered to be mounted upon a lean camel and conducted to the unhappy Shah Allum, whom he had so unmercifully blinded. He bore the dreadful punishment without shrinking — with a heroism, indeed, worthy of a better cause — but expired on his way to Delhi from extreme thirst, brought on by the severity of his sufferings. His inexorable judge had previously ordered that nothing should be given to him either to eat or drink: his death must therefore have been one of intense agony.

Such acts of retribution are in truth fearfully inhuman, but are nevertheless so common under the government of despots that they cease to look upon them with anything but indifference. In their code of equity the great axiom is " an eye for an eye and a tooth for a tooth," and unless this be enforced to the very letter, they consider that justice is not satisfied, and mercy always yields to the sterner attribute.

From this period to 1802, when Lord Lake defeated the successor of the great Scindia six miles from Delhi, and restored the old emperor from the condition of a state-prisoner to that of a free sovereign, the situation of the latter was sad in the extreme. The yearly stipend allowed to each surviving prince of the imperial family did not exceed two hundred rupees, or twenty-two pounds sterling per annum; while the entire amount disbursed on account of the emperor, including his own personal expenses, those of his family and dependants, and of the numerous stipendiaries whom he had to support, did not more than make up the sum of two lacs of rupees, or twenty-four thousand pounds sterling per annum. The seraglio, which is the most expensive portion of the personal establishment of a Mahomedan prince, was reduced to a pitiable condition, and the emperor found himself in his old age without the power of securing the comforts of those who had not the means of realizing their own, and these too the objects of his tenderest affections.

The seraglio of an eastern prince is at once the penetralia of the political and social sanctuary, whence emanate all the cabals and conspiracies so rife in the cabinets of Moslem potentates; it may, therefore, be as well to give a brief description of this part of a Mahomedan sovereign's domestic establishment. In the seraglio are educated the Mogul princes and the principal youth among the nobles destined for posts of responsibility in the empire. It is generally separated from the palace, but so nearly contiguous as to be of ready access. None are admitted within its apartments except the emperor and those immediately attached to its several offices, the duties of which are performed by women. It is generally inclosed by lofty walls and surrounded by spacious gardens, laid out with all the splendour of eastern magnificence, where every luxury is obtained which the appetite may demand or money can procure. Those inmates who form the matrimonial confederacy of the Mogul potentate, are among the most beautiful girls which the empire can furnish. They are taught embroidery, music, and dancing, by certain old women hired to instruct them in every blandishment that may captivate the senses and stimulate the passions. These lovely captives are never permitted to appear abroad, except when the emperor travels, and then they are conveyed in litters closed by curtains, or in boats with small cabins, admitting the light and air only through narrow Venetian blinds.

The apartments of the seraglio are very splendid, always, however, of course in proportion to the wealth of the prince; and the favourite object of his affections exhibits the dignity and enjoys the privileges of a queen, though of a queen in captivity. While her beauty lasts she is frequently regarded with a feeling almost amounting to idolatry; but when that beauty passes away, the warmth of love subsides, her person no longer charms, her voice ceases to impart delight, her faded cheeks and sharpened tones become disagreeable memorials of the past. Neither her song nor her lute are now heard with pleasure, for, in the beautiful imagery of the Persian poet, " When the roses wither and the bower loses its sweetness, you have no longer the tale of the nightingale."

The favourite, however, while she continues her ascendency over the heart of her lord, is treated with sovereign respect throughout the harem. She smokes her golden-tubed hooka, the mouth-piece studded with gems, and enjoys the fresh morning breeze under a verandah that overlooks the gardens of the palace, attended by her damsels, only second to herself in attractions of person and splendour of attire.

> " Her smiling countenance resplendent shines
> With youth and loveliness; her lips disclose

> Teeth white as jasmine blossoms; silky curls
> Luxuriant shade her cheeks, and every limb
> Of slightest texture moves with natural grace,
> Like moonbeams gliding through the yielding air.*

Here she reclines in oblivious repose upon a rich embroidered carpet from the most celebrated looms of Persia. Through an atmosphere of the richest incense she breathes the choicest perfumes of Arabia the happy, and has everything around her that can administer to sensual delight; still she is generally an unhappy being. She dwells in the midst of splendid misery and ungratifying profusion, while all within herself is desolation and hopelessness. Her sympathies are either warped or stifled; her heart is blighted and her mind degraded. She cannot join in the enthusiasm of the inimitable Hafiz†—" the breath of the western gale will soon shed musk around;—the old world will again be young;" but languishes as the seasons return in the most debasing captivity and feels that the western gale breathes not upon her either the freshness of freedom or of joy.

A description of the haram of the celebrated Mogul Emperor Akbar, by the no less celebrated Abul Fazel Mobarek, his minister, will, I trust, be not unwelcome to the reader. " The haram is an enclosure of such an immense extent, as to contain a separate room for every one of the women, whose number exceeds five thousand. They are divided into companies, and a

---

* Uttara Rama Cheritra, a Hindoo drama, translated by Horace Hayman Wilson, Esq. from the original Sanscrit.

† Hafiz was a lyric poet, called by way of pre-eminent distinction, the Anacreon of Persia.

proper employment is assigned to each individual. Over each of these companies a woman is appointed Darogha. And one is selected for the command of the whole, in order that the affairs of the haram may be conducted with the same regularity and good government as the other departments of the state.

Every one receives a salary equal to her merit. The pen cannot measure the extent of the emperor's largesses; but here shall be given some account of the monthly stipend of each. The ladies of the first quality receive from one thousand six hundred and ten rupees, down to one thousand and twenty-eight rupees. Some of the principal servants of the presence have from fifty-one down to twenty rupees, and others are paid from two rupees up to forty.

At the grand gate is stationed a mushreff, to take account of the receipts and expenditures of the haram in ready money and in goods.

Whenever any of this multitude of women want anything, they apply to the treasurer of the haram, who, according to their monthly stipend, sends a memorandum thereof to the mushreff of the grand gate, who transmits it to the treasurer of the king's palace, who pays the money.

The inside of the haram is guarded by women, and about the gate of the royal apartments are placed the most confidential. Immediately on the outside of the gate watch the eunuchs of the haram, and at a proper distance are stationed the Rajpoots, beyond whom are the porters of the gates, and on the outside of the enclosure, the omrahs, the ahdeeans, and other troops mount guard, according to their rank.

Whenever the begums or the wives of the omrahs, or other women of character, want to pay their compliments, they first notify their desire to those who wait on the outside, and from thence their request is sent in writing to the officers of the palace, after which they are permitted to enter the haram. And some women of rank obtain permission to remain there for the space of a month. But besides all the precautions above described, his majesty depends on his own vigilance, as well as on that of his guards."*

* Ayeen Akbery, vol. i. part I.

CHAPTER VII.

NOOR JEHAN.—CHAJA AIASS.—SHERE AFKUN.

It was from the seraglio that the celebrated Noor Jehan, Jehangire's favourite empress, fulminated those decrees—for though they passed in her husband's name, it is creditably attested that they emanated from her—which rendered the reign of Jehangire one of the most politically prosperous in the annals of Mahomedan history. This remarkable woman was as extraordinary in her birth as in her life, in her obscurity as in her exaltation. The whole period of her existence, though so long confined within the walls of a seraglio, was one signal display of intellectual energy, marvellous enterprise, and boundless ambition. She had not only the mind to conceive, but the resolution to act; not only the spirit to undertake, but the fortitude to endure. The peculiar circumstances of her birth form one of the finest episodes in Farishta's history.

This celebrated woman was the daughter of Chaja Aiass, a native of Western Tartary, who was of an ancient and noble race, though under the various vicissitudes of "time and circumstance" his family had sunk into comparative destitution. He therefore quitted his country for Hindostan, hoping under the Mogul emperor to repair the loss of fortune.

Having become enamoured of a young woman, as poor but enthusiastic as himself, he married her. This so incensed his family that they discarded him; when he, under the excitement of indignation at what he considered to be his wrongs, mounted his wife upon an old horse, and walking by her side, proceeded towards the capital of the renowned Akbar. Their scanty supply of money was soon exhausted. They had no means of procuring sustenance, and were apparently fast approaching destruction. They had not tasted food for three days: difficulties every moment accumulated upon them, and to crown their misery the wife of the Tartar was seized with the pains of labour. Assisted only by her wretched husband, she gave birth to a daughter. They were in the midst of a vast desert where the foot of man but seldom penetrated, and had no other prospect but of perishing with hunger or by wild beasts. Chaja Aiass having placed his wife upon the horse as soon as he could do so with safety, found himself unable to follow with the infant. The mother was too weak to carry it, and there was but one alternative. The struggle of nature was a severe one; there was however no choice left between death and parental subjugation. It was agreed by the half distracted parents that the newborn pledge of their affection must be abandoned. They covered it with leaves, and left it in the path to the mercy of that God who can protect the babe in the desert as well as the sovereign on his throne.

The miserable pair pursued their journey in silence and in agony. After a short progress, the invincible yearnings of nature prevailed over the torments of hunger and thirst, and the bereaved mother called distractedly for her child. The heart of the husband was subdued by her sufferings; dashing the tear from his cheek, he undertook to return and restore it to her arms. He retraced his steps, but was paralysed with horror, on arriving at the spot where he had left his infant, to see a large black snake wreathed round it. In a paroxysm of desperation he rushed forward, when the monster, gradually uncoiling itself, retired into the hollow of a tree. He snatched up the child and bore it in ecstasy to the anxious mother. It had received no hurt, and whilst by their caresses they were expressing their exultation at its singular escape, some travellers overtook them, who supplied them with food and enabled them to resume their journey. They advanced by easy stages till they reached Lahore.

Soon after the arrival of the poor Tartar in this city, where the great Akbar then held his court, he was fortunate enough to attract that emperor's attention, and by an extraordinary accession of good fortune became finally high treasurer of the empire. His daughter, as she grew up, excelled all the loveliest women of the East, and was therefore named Mher-ul-Nissa, or the Sun of women. The greatest care was taken to make her mistress of every accomplishment which could impart an additional fascination to the natural graces of her sex. In vivacity, wit, spirit, and all those elegant attainments in which women especially excel, she was equalled by few and surpassed by none. In masculine vigour of understanding she stood alone and unapproached. The emperor's son, Selim, afterwards so well known as the Emperor Jehangire, having seen her, became enamoured of her, and this hasty prepossession the ambitious fair one exerted all her powers to strengthen. In the frenzy of his passion, Prince Selim applied to Akbar for his consent to marry her, but the latter sternly refused it. Shortly after the lovely daughter of Chaja Aiass became the wife of Shere Afkun, a Turkoman noble of high distinction, to whom she had been long betrothed.

Selim was from that moment the bitter foe of his successful rival; he secretly disseminated calumnies to the injury of Shere Afkun, who in disgust retired from court into the province of Bengal, where he obtained from the governor the vicegerency of Burdwan, a considerable district in that province. When Prince Selim became emperor, his passion for the daughter of Aiass revived in full force; the restraint being removed under which the smothered flame had been so long and so painfully suppressed, it burst forth with increased fierceness. He was now absolute, and determined to possess the object of his disappointed love; he therefore made advances towards a reconciliation with Shere Afkun, but the brave Turkoman for a time resisted all his importunities; perceiving their object, and resolving to part neither with his wife nor with his honour, as he could not resign the one without relinquishing the other. His strength was prodigious and his bravery equal to his strength; his integrity was unimpeached, his reputation high, and he was alike feared and respected by all classes. Upon every occasion where danger was imminent he was foremost to encounter it, while his valour was the theme of many a romance and of many a song. His bodily vigour was so great that he had slain a lion single-handed, from which circumstance he obtained the cognomen of Shere Afkun, or the lion-slayer, his original name being Asta Jillo. He had been much esteemed by Akbar, who valued alike his bravery and his virtues.

Soon after Jehangire ascended the imperial throne of the Moguls, Shere Afkun was invited to court, whither, after repeated solicitations, he repaired, trusting to his own high reputation for security against any tyrannical exercise of the sovereign power. Upon his arrival, he was much caressed by the emperor in order to lull suspicion: open and generous himself, he suspected no treachery in others. A day was at length appointed for the chase: the omrahs and inferior nobles assembled, and the forest-haunts of the lion and tiger were explored. The hunters soon inclosed a mighty beast of the latter species, of which the emperor being apprised, immediately proceeded to the spot. He demanded of those around him who would venture to attack it: all stood silent and confounded. Shere Afkun began to hope that the enterprise would devolve upon him, when three omrahs stepped forward and offered to encounter the forest tyrant. The pride of the bold Turkoman was roused; they had challenged the encounter, and he therefore could not set aside their prior claim to the distinction which they insisted upon striving for. Shere Afkun, fearing that he was likely to be rivalled and that his fame would thus be tarnished, advanced and presenting himself before the emperor, said firmly, " To attack an unarmed creature with weapons is neither fair nor manly. The Deity has given limbs and sinews to man as well as to tigers, and has imparted reason to the former in order to countervail the deficiency of strength."

The omrahs declined such a perilous contest, when the bold warrior, to the emperor's surprise and delight, instantly cast aside his weapon and his shield and prepared to engage the tiger unarmed. The encounter is described with the most appalling minuteness by the Mogul historians. After a desperate conflict, and mangled by terrific wounds, the heroic Afkun forced his arm down the throat of his adversary, grasped him firmly by the root of the tongue and finally strangled him. Thus were the secret expectations of Jehangire defeated, and the fame of this extraordinary exploit resounded through the empire.

Shere had scarcely recovered, when private orders were given to the driver of a large elephant to waylay him and tread him to death. He saw the elephant approach; the street was narrow and there were no means of escape. Perceiving his danger, he ordered his bearers to turn, but they threw down the palankeen and fled. The Turkoman undismayed sprang instantly upon his feet, drew his sword, and before the elephant could accomplish its fatal purpose, severed its trunk close to the root. The huge animal immediately dropped and expired. Jehangire witnessed the action. He had placed himself at a small lattice that overlooked the street. He was perfectly amazed, but disappointment and vexation banished from his bosom the better feelings of his nature. Shere Afkun waited upon the emperor, and communicated to him what he had done. Jehangire extolled his bravery with warmth, and thus escaped the hero's suspicion.

He was not however permitted to remain long unmolested. Kuttub, suba or governor of Bengal, knowing his master's wishes and in order to ensure his further favour, hired forty ruffians to assassinate the dreaded omrah. So confident was the latter in his own strength and valour that he took no precaution to protect himself either against secret or open enemies. He retained only an old porter in his house, all his other servants occupying apartments at a distance. The assassins entered his room where their victim was asleep, when one of them, touched with remorse, cried out, "Hold! are we men? What! forty to one and afraid to encounter him awake!" The Turkoman, aroused by this timely and manly expostulation, started from his bed, seized his sword, and retiring backward before the assassins had all entered, reached the corner of the apartment, where he prepared to defend himself to the last extremity. The ruffians, fearing their victim would escape, rushed on him so tumultuously that they encumbered each other. Shere Afkun, taking advantage of their confusion, laid several of them dead at his feet; many others fell desperately wounded and the rest betook themselves to flight. The man who had warned the hero of his danger, stood fixed in mute astonishment at the prowess of him whom he had been hired to murder. His intended victim advanced, and kindly taking his hand, welcomed him as his deliverer.

Having ascertained from the man's unreluctant confession by whom the assassins had been hired, he dismissed him with a liberal benefaction.

This remarkable exploit was repeated from mouth to mouth with a thousand exaggerations, so that whenever Shere Afkun appeared abroad, he was followed and pointed at as a man of superhuman powers; but in order to avoid the recurrence of perils similar to those from which he had so recently escaped, he retired to Burdwan.

Meanwhile the suba of Bengal had received the emperor's orders to despatch this extraordinary man, but dared not openly execute them. Coming with a great retinue to Burdwan, about sixty miles from the modern capital of this extensive province, under pretence of making a tour of the territory placed under his political superintendence, he communicated to his principal officers the secret of his mission. The devoted omrah went out to meet the suba as he was entering the town, and the latter affected to treat him with great cordiality. In the progress of the cavalcade, a pikeman, pretending that Shere Afkun was in the way, rudely struck his horse. The indignant noble, knowing that no soldier would have done this without orders, immediately saw that his life was aimed at, and directly spurred his horse towards the elephant of the treacherous suba, tore down the howda and slew the cowardly Kuttub before any of his guards could rescue him: then turning upon the omrahs, five were almost instantly sacrificed to his just revenge.

Terrified at his prowess, the soldiers began to discharge their arrows and muskets at him from a distance; his horse, struck by a ball in the forehead, fell dead under him. Covered with wounds and bleeding at every pore, the still undaunted lion-slayer called on the suba's officers to advance and meet him in single combat, but they, one and all, declined the encounter. At length, seeing his end approaching, the brave Turkoman, like a devout Mahomedan, turned his face towards Mecca, threw some dust upon his head by way of ablution, there being no water near, and standing up calm and undismayed before the armed files of his murderers, received at one discharge six balls in his body and expired without a groan.

The beautiful widow was immediately transported to Delhi, but Jehangire refused to see her, whether from remorse or policy is uncertain. He ordered her to be confined in one of the worst apartments of the seraglio. The daughter of the Tartar Aiass was a woman of haughty spirit and could ill brook this indifference. It preyed deeply upon her mind. Meanwhile she was not idle. Being very expert at working tapestry and all kinds of embroidery, and in painting silks with the richest devices, she applied herself with great assiduity to those employments. In a short time the exquisite productions of her taste and skill became the talk of the capital. The ladies of the omrahs of Delhi and Agra would wear nothing on grand occasions but what came from the hands of the beautiful Mher-ul-Nissa. She therefore soon became the oracle of fashion and of taste. Whilst she affected an extreme simplicity in her own dress, she attired her attendants in the richest tissues and brocades, making those who had attractive persons the vehicles for setting off to advantage the works of her own industry. She thus amassed a considerable sum of money, and became more celebrated in her obscurity than she had hitherto been as the wife of the most distinguished hero of his age. Her milder glories had been hitherto eclipsed by the predominancy of his.

The accomplishments of this singular woman were soon carried to the ears of the emperor, who had probably by this time forgotten the ascendency which she once held over his heart. He determined therefore to see her in order to have ocular proof whether the voice of public report was a truth or an exaggeration. Resolving to take her by surprise, he unexpectedly entered her apartment, when, at the sight of her unrivalled beauty, all his former passion revived in an instant. She was reclining on a sofa in an undress robe of plain white muslin which exhibited her faultless shape to the best advantage, and became her better than the richest brocades of Bagdat, or the finest embroideries of Cashmere. As soon as the emperor entered, the syren rose with an agitation that served only to heighten her charms, and fixed her eyes on the ground with well-dissembled confusion. Jehangire stood mute with amazement; rapture took immediate possession of his soul; he felt, if he did not utter, the sentiment of an emiment poet of his own religion—

> Sweet maid, if thou wouldst charm my sight,
> And bid these arms thy neck infold;
> That rosy cheek, that lily hand,
> Would give thy lover more delight
> Than all Bocâra's vaunted gold—
> Than all the gems of Sarmacand.*

He was dazzled by the perfection of her form, the dignity of her mien, and the transcendent loveliness of her features. Advancing to where she stood in the plenitude of her beauty, he took her hand, declared his resolution to make her his empress, and immediately a proclamation was issued for the celebration of the royal nuptials with the lovely relict of the late Shere Afkun.

The name of Mher-ul-Nissa was exchanged for that of Noor Mahil—"the light of the harem." From this moment she became the favourite wife of the sovereign of the Moguls. In the climax of her exaltation her name was again changed to Noor Jehan, or, "the light of the world." As a distinguishing mark of her pre-eminence in the emperor's affections, she was allowed to assume the title of Shahe, or empress. The current coin was stamped with her name as well as with the sovereign's. Her family was held next in rank to the princes of the blood, and advanced to places of the highest trust. Its members were admitted to privileges which had never before been enjoyed by subjects under the Mogul domination. Her influence exceeded that of any person in the empire, not even excepting the emperor; and perhaps under the rigid scrupulosity of Mogul policy with

---

* Hafiz, translated by Sir Wm. Jones.

regard to women sharing in the administration of the state, there never has been an instance of one of the sex attaining an ascendency so paramount, and such perfect political control over the destinies of so many subject principalities as the renowned Noor Jehan.

CHAPTER VIII.

DELHI.—TOGLOKABAD.—A HINDOO TEMPLE.

We saw much more of Delhi on our return than on our upward journey; for we made a longer stay there. One of the most striking objects in the modern city, though by no means one of the most magnificent, is the tomb of Sufter Jung, a Mahomedan chieftain of some repute, who died about the middle of the last century. This structure is ranked among the best architectural works of New Delhi. It is surrounded by a large garden, enclosed by a high wall, above which the dome and minor cupolas of the edifice appear with agreeable effect, when beheld from the plain without. The body of the building is composed of light red stone tessellated with white marble, beautifully contrasting its pure bright surface with the dull red of the mass which forms the monument. The dome is entirely of white marble, rising majestically over the body of the edifice, and relieved against a clear blue sky which seems to be its native element, as if it were the aërial abode of some guardian angel watching the slumbers of the dead, reduced to its primitive dust in a capacious sarcophagus below. The entrance into the gardens is through a handsome square building, in which are apartments for the different stipendiaries. In the right hand corner there is an elegant mosque, and in the left a small pavilion. These gardens have suffered greatly from neglect. They are of considerable extent and inspire a solemn impression as you enter, which is no doubt enhanced by the desolation that seems to reign around. The mind is irresistibly impressed with a feeling that it is the abode of silence and of death. There is a perception imparted, and a sentiment realized, of which we are perhaps never so conscious as when we draw nigh to " the place of graves," where " the prisoners rest together, and hear not the voice of the oppressor."

Before we quitted this neighbourhood, we visited the fort of Toglokabad, at the extremity of one of the Mewat hills, not far from the city. It was erected by Toglok Shah, a Patan prince of some celebrity, in the early part of the ninth century. It is built in a bold style, its massy walls bidding defiance to all the means of assault practised at that early period; though it is pretended that the use of fire-arms was known in India some time previously to the first irruption of the Moguls into Hindostan, three centuries before its invasion by Timour, when that portion of the peninsula between the Indus and the Ganges, to which his family so rapidly succeeded, was under the Patan, or Afghan government: so that cannon might have been in use when this fort was erected—indeed the strength of its defences would imply that even in that early age sieges had already become formidable.

The tomb of the founder is seen near the fort, and

is built of the same materials, in a plain unpretending style, but with the same massive strength. Though rudely constructed and almost entirely without ornament, it is nevertheless not deficient in general grandeur of effect, which is somewhat increased by the natural solitariness and asperity of the spot.

Near the tomb, we entered a temple, in which were several small brass images, such as are commonly sold for a few rupees in the bazaars. We were attended by one of the officiating Brahmins, who was exceedingly courteous and more than usually communicative. The temple is but a rude structure, and the attendant functionaries appear to be miserably poor, living upon the small gratuities of devotees who casually resort to this humble sanctuary. They were very civil and showed us every part of the building without the slightest hesitation. They manifested none of that reluctance to answer any questions respecting their worship, which is generally shown by the better-conditioned ministers of those sanctuaries that are more richly endowed. Everything here bespoke extreme poverty, and if the spiritual attendants were devout in proportion, they must indeed have been most holy men.

Before we quitted this temple, a circumstance occurred which strikingly displayed the selfish and equivocal casuistry of the mercenary Hindoo. I happened to take a fancy to one of the little brazen gods which was placed upon a sort of altar in the most sacred part of the edifice. It was a very clumsy cast in brass, but one which I had never before seen, and was therefore anxious to possess. Knowing that

these deities had been occasionally sold by the Brahmins from their very altars, I proposed to purchase this, and made for it what I imagined to be a very liberal offer. The obsequious priest, bowing his head, placed his hand upon his breast with the most ludicrous humility, and said that he could not sell, since that would be a desecration of the holy sanctuary of which he was an unworthy minister, and that he could not give because he was too poor to replace the treasure of which the temple would be thus deprived; but, he continued, " suppose sahib take, what can a poor Brahmin do?" Upon this hint I acted, and, without the slightest opposition from the good-tempered priest, took possession of the image. The holy man did not even offer a rebuke, but, on the contrary, extended his open palm towards me, into which I dropped a pagoda that I had previously held between my finger and thumb, and upon which he closed his hand with a courteous smile, bowing with the profoundest reverence the moment his flesh felt the delectable pressure of the gold.

It is surprising to see with what facility some of these spiritual functionaries reconcile themselves to a breach of the spirit of their religious restrictions, though they literally conform to them. The obligation of sincerity is, with a large portion of them, a mere dead letter; so much so that they claim the rewards of heavenly beatitude, if they outwardly obey a given law, whatever depravity may lurk in the heart. It is true that such mental reservations or compromises of conscience are not admitted by the more intelligent of their priesthood as legitimately moral feelings, nor as sanctioned by the spirit of their religion. Those Brahmins, who are really learned, and such are by no means uncommon, have a nice perception of moral influence. They teach the doctrines of a refined practical philosophy, contending for inward purity and integrity of heart as well as for external decorum of conduct, and there are many among them of very rare mental endowments. We find, moreover, many axioms of a high morality among their religious and philosophical writings. I take one at random from the Institutes of Menu. "Let not a man be querulous even though in pain; let him not injure another in deed or in thought; let him not even utter a word by which his fellow-creature may suffer uneasiness; since that will obstruct his own progress to future beatitude."* There is a beautiful maxim quoted by Sir William Jones, and written upwards of three hundred years before the Christian era, which would do honour to any religious community — it pronounces the duty of a good man, even in the moment of destruction, to consist, "not only in forgiving but even in a desire to benefit, his destroyer, as the sandal-tree, in the instant of its overthrow, sheds perfume on the axe that fells it." These are the suggestions of no common minds, and whoever, in seeking to ascertain the Hindoo character, shall judge of it from those with whom he may happen to come in contact, in passing rapidly through any part of their country, will be sure to look at it through a false medium and consequently not appreciate it justly. If there be much to despise, there is

* Institutes of Menu, chap. 2, on Education.

also much to admire. It cannot indeed be denied that many of their religious teachers are so ignorant as to uphold the most barbarous superstitions, which of course are eagerly received by the deluded multitude; but it is equally true, that in almost every age of the world, they have produced learned men among them who would have done honour to any country and at any period.

During our stay at Delhi, we took advantage of our leisure, and saw everything in the city worth the traveller's attention. I shall, therefore, enter a little further into detail concerning one or two of the more remarkable buildings of this still magnificent city. The gateways of the fort are built in a style sufficiently bold, but look heavy in consequence of the material being a dull red stone. In two or three of these gateways there are marks of the severity of Gholaum Kaudir's cannonading, before he was obliged to fly from the scene of his atrocities by the victorious Scindia, who visited him with so horrible a retribution. In the first court there is a cannon of so vast a calibre that a large man may lie in it with ease. I believe it is now never fired. In the second court is the Dewan Aum, or hall of public audience. The musnud* upon which the Mogul emperors once sat was a most costly piece of work. It was in the form of a peacock with the tail outspread, entirely composed of diamonds and other precious stones. It had been valued at seven millions sterling. This gorgeous piece of state furniture was taken away by that rapacious spoiler Nadir Shah, and since the

* Mahomedan throne.

period of this predal abomination, the emperors of Delhi have been content to sit upon a much less costly throne.

In the third court is the Dewan Kauss, or hall of private audience, built entirely of marble, and richly ornamented with representations of various flowers. This is a very elegant structure, and the interior scarcely less costly than that of the Dewan Aum. Over the arches which support the roof is the following inscription in Persian characters, beautifully inlaid with silver on a ground of dark but brilliantly polished marble:—" If there be a heaven on earth, it is here, it is here, it is here." The characters are large and admirably formed; indeed, I think it is the finest specimen of the Persian text I ever witnessed. In this hall there was an immense block of crystal, on which the unhappy Shah Allum always used to sit when he held a private audience of his ministers. Its superficial measurement was four feet by three, and it was eighteen inches thick. The apartment formerly devoted to the royal privacy, into which no one was permitted to intrude but upon business of great moment, is close by the Dewan Kauss. It was gorgeously furnished. Over it is a gilt dome, the most spacious in the palace. The gardens are now quite in ruins. In the centre is a large square basin, said to have been originally lined with crystal. It contains gold and silver fish. Close by it there was a marble seat for the emperor's use when he chose to visit the gardens. At a short distance was a large bath, much like a huge sarcophagus, cut out of the solid marble. Between the garden and the Dewan Kauss are the royal baths; they are composed entirely of marble and elaborately embellished, the floors and sides being elegantly inlaid with flowers of variously coloured stones.

A few days after our arrival at Delhi a male elephant, having killed its driver, escaped from its stable and, running through the city in a state of great excitement, created considerable alarm. The enraged animal, when it got outside the walls, stood eyeing the approaching multitude which had followed it from the town, with a most mischievous expression and a very sinister motion of the proboscis. Its look was so determined that no one had the courage to approach, when an English soldier from a small detachment on its march to Cawnpore, rendered more than usually courageous from having indulged in liberal potations of arrack, advanced with the most undaunted bearing towards the angry animal, which calmly awaited his approach. The spectators imagined that instant destruction must be the issue of this mad freak. On the contrary, to the astonishment of all present, the elephant permitted the drunken soldier to seize it by the trunk with impunity, bent its knees and inclined its head to enable the man to mount, who, assisted by the animal, now no longer refractory, got upon its neck and drove it into the city amid the acclamations of the crowd, by whom it was finally secured.

After we quitted this interesting capital of a once flourishing but now subverted empire, on passing by Feroz Shah's cotilla,* a few leagues from Delhi, our

* A fortified house.

attention was arrested by a pillar composed of a single stone forty-six feet high and upwards of ten in circumference at the base. It is said to have been much more lofty, a large portion of it having been struck down by lightning many years since, without shattering any part of the column below. The top of the shaft bears evident marks of severe injury, and the story has decidedly the voucher of strong external evidences in favour of its truth. It certainly has the appearance of a broken column. The whole has a fine polish until within a few feet of the base, where the curious and the lovers of virtu have clipped it off; the one to satisfy an idle curiosity in ascertaining if it were really stone, the other to add an item to his choice collection of extraordinary fragments. How often have the finest monuments of man's mental and manual labour been thus dilapidated to make a valueless addition to a collection of lumber!

This remarkable pillar has been supposed by many to be nothing more than a composition which time has compacted into a mass so solid as to give it the appearance of a hard impenetrable granite; but there are no just grounds for such a supposition, since the stratifications may be distinctly traced, and it has all the compactness of marble with a like capability of receiving the most exquisite polish. There are several inscriptions upon this pillar which it has baffled the ingenuity of the learned to decipher. They are perfectly legible, but the character is not recognized, so that the column must be of extreme antiquity.

As the day was unusually hot, we were much gratified just at the entrance of a small village at seeing a fruitstall, on which there was no despicable display of some of the choicest fruits which this fine climate produces. It was a shed very rudely constructed, thatched with long wiry grass, and supported by four slender bamboos. The front was open, but the back was covered by a light frame of bamboo thatched like the roof, while a coarse drapery hung down on one side. The girl who presided over this rude pavilion of the Indian Pomona, was a prepossessing young Hindoo, the graceful flower of sixteen summers!

> Arched is her brow like heaven's gay bow of light,
> Her gentle breast heaves lovely to the sight,
> With the bright moon her brighter face may vie,
> And with the lotus' purest tint her eye.
> Her step the elephant's proud gait reveals,
> And sweetness from the cygnet's * voice she steals.

She was leaning with her back against the stand on which some of her fruits were disposed for sale in tempting profusion, while at her feet lay a basket of pine apples and bananas. She pressingly but gracefully invited us to become purchasers of the choicest of her stock, for which she courteously asked us about ten times its value; but who could refuse what was so eloquently demanded by this interesting creature? We bought the best of what she had to offer, and paid her without reluctance what she demanded, which gave her, no doubt, an idea that we were more liberal than wise.†

* The Hindoos have a fabulous bird so called, which is said to feed on pearls, and whose voice is most melodious.
† See title page.

CHAPTER IX.

THE CHAUTER SERAI.—A VICIOUS CAMEL.

We now followed the course of the Jumna to the Chauter Serai, built by Asuf Khan, brother to the celebrated Noor Jehan. From the top of it the eye embraces a very extensive and agreeable prospect. It is said to be one of the finest serais in the country, and is in excellent repair. The gateway is particularly elegant, and seen from the distance as you approach upon a gentle ascent, flanked on either side by a lofty parapeted wall, the effect is extremely picturesque. The area within the walls is of great extent and is generally found occupied by travellers. Its recesses are so numerous as to afford accommodation to a large number. There is moreover an extensive bazaar in the neighbourhood, so that they have no difficulty in procuring anything they may require.

The morning after our halt at this interesting spot, Mr. Daniell and myself rose early in order to indulge ourselves with a sight of the beautiful prospect around us. The sun had just risen; the distant hills were tinged with its beams, but the gloom of twilight was still in the valleys. As the gate of the serai stood upon a considerable elevation, the sun's rays were intercepted by it; but slanting through the portal they fell brightly upon the busy travellers who had just resumed their journey down the winding path that led from their welcome shelter, imparting a most delightful feature to the scene. There was a delicious freshness in the morning, and I could not refrain from wishing the travellers a hearty " God speed!"

A small detachment of European troops, on their way to Delhi, halted here a few hours after sunrise. We joined the two officers who accompanied it, and this casual meeting of our countrymen was a very agreeable incident in our long though interesting journey. The detachment consisted of about seventy men, under the command of a lieutenant, accompanied by a junior officer. They had pitched their tent within a small grove at a short distance from the serai walls, while the soldiers were quietly reposing under the deep shade of the trees. The elephants, camels, and other cattle were picketed around them. Whilst the detachment was preparing for its march on the following morning, an accident happened, which I relate, as it will serve to show the disposition of that very useful, but occasionally savage creature, the camel. In general, indeed, this animal is remarkably tractable, kneeling down at the slightest intimation of its keeper, quietly ruminating while the latter loads it, and patiently submitting to the imposition of a very heavy burthen. One of the camels, however, belonging to the troops preparing to proceed on their march, contrary to its usual habit, refused to obey the command of its driver, and stood motionless in stubborn defiance of authority. The man tugged in vain at the cord passed through its nostrils, which is the mode of bridling the camel, when a soldier, impatient at the delay, advanced and struck the animal a violent blow on the knee with the handle of his bayonet. The mild spirit of the camel was instantly converted into the most implacable hostility. Its eyes flashed fire; its nostrils expanded; it stamped, projected its ears, and snorted violently. The expression of its fury was indescribable. The soldier heeded not this fearful menace, but repeated the blow. The creature's eyes now dilated to an intense stare, assuming at the same moment a glare of the most deadly ferocity; bending down its head, its jaws distended and its lips quivering with rage, it seized the soldier by the arm between the elbow and the shoulder, raised him in the air, snapping the bone in an instant, shook him furiously, then dashed him upon the ground, and was preparing to repeat the punishment, when the wounded man was rescued by some of his comrades, and the camel secured. It would not, however, suffer itself to be loaded, and was led forward by the driver, the baggage which it should have borne being divided between the less turbulent of its fellow beasts of burthen.

Shortly after the departure of our military companions, I took my gun and proceeded into a neighbouring wood in search of game, and as I was standing near a spot thickly overgrown with short bushes, the native attendant who accompanied me suddenly gave an exclamation of alarm, pointing at my feet and exhibiting at the same time, every symptom of extreme terror. Perfectly unconscious of the cause of

his sudden excitement, I cast my eyes on the ground in the direction towards which he pointed, and to my consternation saw a large cobra snake actually gliding between my feet with the most quiet deliberation. For a moment I felt paralysed. In fact, I was too much alarmed to stir; but in the course of a few seconds the reptile passed harmlessly on its way, and escaped into the thicket. Had I been more collected, I probably should have fired at it; but my energies were so completely overcome at the moment, that this never once occurred to my mind, though as soon as the snake was out of sight, I confess I did entertain the somewhat ungenerous regret that I had not destroyed it. I was however no longer disposed to continue my search after game, but returned to the serai, where I felt not the slightest disposition to demur at seeing a chicken served up for dinner instead of a roasted partridge or peacock.

It is generally imagined, and by persons too who have been some time resident in India, that the Cobra di Capello exhibited by the jugglers in this country, is perfectly harmless, in consequence of its fangs being extracted by these practised adepts in the art of legerdemain; but this is altogether a mistake. The fangs are positively not extracted, and the creature is presented to the spectator possessing all its natural powers of mischief unimpaired. The bite from a snake shown by any of these itinerant conjurors would as certainly prove fatal as from one encountered in the jungle. This will, perhaps, appear strange to those who have heard of these reptiles being constantly shown in the houses of the curious, and more especially when they are told that this snake is frequently permitted to put its head against the cheeks of the children of those who show them.

The dexterity of the jugglers in managing these dangerous reptiles is truly extraordinary. They easily excite them to the most desperate rage, and by a certain circular motion of the arms appease them as readily; then without the least hesitation they will take them in their hands, coil them round their necks, and put their fingers to their mouths, even while their jaws are furnished with the deadliest venom, and the slightest puncture from their fangs would produce not only certain but almost instant death.

The power which these people exercise over this species of venomous snake remains no longer a mystery when its habits are known. It is a remarkable peculiarity in the Cobra di Capello, and, I believe, in most poisonous reptiles of this class, that they have an extreme reluctance to put into operation the deadly powers with which they are endowed. The cobra scarcely ever bites unless excited by actual injury or extreme provocation, and even then before it darts upon its aggressor it always gives him timely notice of his danger not to be mistaken. It dilates the crest upon its neck, which is a large flexible membrane having on the upper surface two black circular spots like a pair of spectacles, waves its head to and fro with a gentle undulatory motion, the eye sparkling with intense lustre, and commences a hiss so loud as to be heard at a considerable distance: so that the juggler always has warning when it is perilous to approach his captive. The snake never bites while the hood is closed, and so long as this is not erected, it may be approached and handled with impunity. Even when the hood is spread, while the creature continues silent, there is no danger. Its fearful hiss is at once the signal of aggression and of peril.

Though the cobra is so deadly when under excitement, it is nevertheless astonishing to see how readily it is appeased even in the highest state of exasperation, and this merely by the droning music with which its exhibitors seem to charm it. It appears to be fascinated by the discordant sounds that issue from their pipes and tomtoms.

I confess, for some time after my arrival in India, I laboured under the general delusion that the fangs of these reptiles were always drawn by the persons who carried them about, and had often fearlessly ventured within their spring with a feeling of entire security; I however took especial care never to approach a captive snake, after I discovered that it still retained its powers of destruction. The jugglers, who gain a precarious subsistence by showing these creatures, will bring them in from the jungles by the neck, and an instance of their being bitten is scarcely ever heard of. They themselves appear not to have the slightest apprehension of danger, for it is not often that the snake, though so rudely seized, manifests any symptoms of irritation.

We were induced to extend our halt near the Chauter Serai in consequence of a hunting party having arrived in the neighbourhood, which we gladly availed ourselves of the opportunity of joining. We proceeded towards the jungle soon after daylight, and having arrived at the appointed place, at least fifty men were sent in to beat the wood, and by yells to scare the game from the cover. They had not been so employed above a quarter of an hour when a large tiger darted from its concealment into the plain. One of the beaters who had previously emerged from the jungle, happened to be standing close to the spot whence the tiger issued, and seeing the enemy so near and in an evident state of furious excitement, fled in terror. The tiger immediately pursued him, and, soon overtaking his affrighted victim, struck him a gentle tap, as it appeared, on the back and passed on. The man instantly fell, rolled on the ground and declared that he was dying. Our general impression was that he could not be seriously hurt from the slight blow he had received; we therefore imputed his cries to fright, especially as there was no perceptible wound on his body, and took it for granted that in an hour or two he would be on his legs again. He was immediately put under the charge of some followers, who were ordered to convey him to the tents without delay.

Meanwhile the tiger was vigorously pursued; being soon surrounded, it at length stopped panting against a bank and prepared to resent the advance of the first adversary. It was so perplexed by the yells of the numerous attendants that it made no further effort to escape, though it had not run above a quarter of a mile from the place where it first broke cover. We were now in an open part of the jungle whither the animal had run for protection from its pursuers; but the party was so numerous and dispersed, that the tiger had not time to penetrate the thicket before it was surrounded and forced to prepare for defence. The grass was high, which a good deal impeded the movements of the shikarries and elephants. These latter were much frightened, on seeing the fierce determination of the enemy towards which the mahoots were violently urging them, and shrank back with their trunks raised in the air, betokening the violence of their alarm. The tiger stood with its eyes glaring upon them, lashing its tail, protruding its claws, every now and then showing its monstrous fangs, uttering a suppressed yell, and exhibiting all those indications of rage so terrible in this ferocious creature.

The elephants remained stationary. Not one of them would advance: on the contrary, several turned their backs upon the infuriated beast and started off at full speed in spite of the efforts of the mahoots to keep them in the field. The tiger did not attempt to move, but maintained its position, eyeing with a deadly ferocity the formidable array by which it was surrounded. At length, after violent exertions on the part of the driver, an old and well-trained male elephant was induced to approach the savage foe. He rushed forward on a sudden, and at the same moment, ere the tiger could make its spring, a shikarry shot it through the body: it staggered and reeled backward. The elephant instantly seized the opportunity, and impaled it with his tusks, pinning it firmly to the earth; but in its death-struggle the enraged brute inflicted so dreadful a laceration on his trunk, that a man's arm, from the elbow downward, could have been laid in the wound.

When the tiger was despatched it was placed upon the back of the victorious elephant, which seemed to proceed under the burthen with conscious triumph; but so terrified were some of its companions that they would not approach their foe, even though it was dead. The victor however marched on in the pride of conscious pre-eminence, and as soon as we regained our tents, for the day's sport was now concluded, the lifeless enemy was unstrapped and immediately rolled upon the ground. The elephants formed a circle round it, though none could be induced to advance within a hundred yards of the gored body. At length the old elephant, in derision of their terror, as it seemed, raised the dead tiger upon one of its tusks and hurled it into the air with as much ease as if it had been a sucking cub. Away they scampered when they saw the dreaded projectile in rapid impulse towards them, and it was with considerable difficulty that the mahoots, after much coaxing, could induce them to return.

Meanwhile the poor fellow who had been wounded continued to complain of great internal suffering, but his protestations were unheeded, as it is too frequently the habit of these people to affect suffering in order to excite compassion and thus obtain money. He was therefore little attended to, more especially as he happened to be a pariah; for the unhappy wretches who bear that designation are looked upon with abhorrence by the higher castes of Hindoos. His complainings procured him no pity, not even from those of his own tribe; there being but little sympathy where there is only a community of wretchedness. Extreme misery always makes us selfish. Everything then merges in the one absorbing feeling of conscious bereavement.

There happened to be a young regimental surgeon of the party, but, either from inexperience or carelessness, he assured us there was nothing the matter and that the man was only frightened. To our surprise the poor fellow died in the course of the night. Upon examining his back more attentively, it became evident that a wound, although a minute one, had been inflicted by the tiger's claw. The young surgeon, now conscious of his mistake, opened the body, when it was found that the claw had pierced through the spine and punctured the intestines:—the complaints of the poor man were at once fully accounted for. I confess that this melancholy issue of the day's sport did not tend to increase my relish for tiger-hunting, and I could not help observing with a painful emotion with what apathy the death of a fellow-creature was regarded.

Eagerly as tiger-hunting is pursued in India, it is nevertheless a dangerous sport. In proof of this I may mention an accident which happened during the Marquis of Hastings's administration. Two young officers were beating a jungle upon an elephant, when a large tiger suddenly sprang upon the animal's flank, reached the seat on which the officers were sitting, and seizing one of them by the thigh instantly dragged him to the ground. He had fortunately the presence of mind to hold the ferocious brute tightly by the ear with one hand, and with the other, drawing a pistol from his pocket, he discharged it into the tiger's belly. The enraged animal, however, continued to drag him onward, until exhausted by loss of blood, it relaxed its gripe ; some of the party coming to their friend's assistance, the tiger was despatched and the officer rescued from jeopardy, though not without being dreadfully lacerated. His life was for some time despaired of, but he happily recovered, and the Marquis of Hastings, as a mark of respect for his intrepidity, placed him upon the staff.

CHAPTER X.

ABDULNUBBI KHAN—MOSQUE AT MATHURA.

I SHOULD have mentioned that at the small town of Furreedabad, between Delhi and the Chauter Serai, we had an opportunity of witnessing the process of bow-making, at which the workmen are there very expert, and the skill displayed by some of them in the use of this weapon is truly astonishing. I have seen a pigeon on the wing struck down by a bowman, and a hare killed at full speed. Nor are such instances of dexterity at all uncommon.

The bows manufactured at Furreedabad are composed of mulberry wood and buffalo's horn, bound with the sinews of the same animal dipped in a strong glue made from the hoof. These bows are in much request. They are very neatly finished, and any one unused to the operation requires great strength of arm to string them. The arrow is a straight reed tipped with a steel barb and feathered at the reverse end. It is thirty-two or three inches long, and the shaft about the third of an inch in diameter. One of the most celebrated marksmen of the place gave us a specimen of his dexterity by striking, at the distance of twenty paces, a small copper coin from the top of a slight bamboo fixed into the ground. He knocked the copper from the bamboo three times out of five. The mark was covered with a piece of white linen in order to render it the more visible. While I am on this subject I may remark that in the island of Madagascar the natives exhibit equal dexterity in hurling the segaï, or javelin. They will pierce an ox through the heart at the distance of twelve yards. I once saw this done three time successively. The last ox was opened, and I stood by during the process, when the head of the spear was found buried in the animal's heart. The weapon used on this occasion was a light javelin with a thin ebony shaft about the thickness of a mould candle of the largest size, having a small steel head of an elliptical shape not barbed, but edged on two sides and very sharp.

Upon quitting the Chauter Serai we reached Mathura, a town celebrated for an establishment of monkeys, supported by a bequest from Mahadajee Scindia, as stated in the former volume of this work. Here is a very magnificent mosque, said to have been built by Abdulnubbi Khan, a foujdar* of the Emperor Aurungzebe. The account given of its origin is somewhat singular. Mathura was at that time, as it has been ever since, a place of much resort by the votaries of Krishna. On the invasion of Mahmood of Ghizni, the celebrated Mahomedan conqueror, in 1018, Mathura was taken and razed to the

---

* The foujdar is an officer who has the charge of a troop of elephants. "The foujdar's business is to teach the elephants to be bold, and not to be frightened at the sight of fire or at the noise of artillery, and he is answerable for their discipline in these respects."—Ayeen Akbery, vol. i. part I.

ground by the haughty warrior, in consequence of the abominable idolatries there practised. Mahmood was a fierce iconoclast, and found abundant exercise for his intolerant zeal, the fury of which he poured out upon this devoted city. It was subsequently rebuilt with much superior magnificence, being embellished with several splendid temples and other ornaments of art which rendered it a place of even greater celebrity than it had formerly been. Krishna was worshipped in still more gorgeous temples, and the number of his votaries had been gradually increasing since the destruction of his shrine by the unrelenting Mahmood.

It is said that Abdulnubbi Khan was seduced from his spiritual allegiance to the prophet of Mecca, and persuaded to offer his oblations on the altar of the Hindoo god. He was detected in the act of prostration before the Pagan image and the circumstance forthwith reported to Aurungzebe, who, being a perfect fanatic in the observance of religious austerities, was highly scandalized at a Mussulmaun degrading himself by so preposterous a fealty. The convicted neophyte, soon convinced of the folly of his proselytism to such a degrading superstition, returned to the spiritual service of the Prophet, and, in order to regain the emperor's favour, pulled down the sanctuary of the god to whom he had so lately dedicated his homage, and raised a mosque on its site. The mosque, however, of which a most faithful representation is given in the accompanying engraving, is stated by some historians, who question the fact just related, to have been built by the emperor himself with the materials of a temple previously erected by the Rajah of Oorcha. This latter is said to have been a noble Hindoo structure raised by the Rajah after the rebuilding of Mathura, and to have cost upwards of four hundred thousand pounds sterling—a vast sum at that period, especially where the price of labour is so low. This was the temple that was pulled down to make room for the mosque, which now stands upon the same ground and is a fine structure. The body of the building, which is quadrangular, is flanked by four superb minarets nearly a hundred feet high. They have each ten angles, are sparingly ornamented and surmounted by small cupolas, supported upon slender pillars of stone. At intervals there are balconies, which are reached by a staircase from within and impart a graceful finish to each minaret. The gateway of this temple is lofty, and its architectural decorations are very elegant. The spandrels of the arch which forms the portal, are faced with white marble, admirably harmonizing with the darker material of which the adjacent parts are constructed. The arch, like the gothic, terminates in a point, rising to a considerable height above the entrance and leading immediately into the interior of the sanctuary. There is a projecting stone gallery over the gateway, decorated with a profusion of tracery in the very happiest style of redundant embellishment; for though the ornaments are profuse, there is not the slightest confusion nor the least violation of taste. On either side of this gallery are sunken panels covered with finely executed inscriptions from the Koran.

From the doorway of the mosque to the street

there is a descent by a broad flight of steps, composed of durable stone, forming at once a compact and beautiful piece of masonry. The street is here so spacious that a numerous cavalcade of elephants and horses may pass without difficulty. The picture represents an elephant kneeling at the bottom of the steps awaiting its rider, who has just descended from his devotions in the sanctuary. On the left of the steps, as you face the mosque, is a large bazaar, abundantly supplied with every thing that might tempt the palate of the most luxurious, from a kismish* to a pine-apple.

In the fort of Mathura are still to be seen the ruins of an observatory, reported to have been a lofty and elegant structure, though, it must be confessed, there are few indications of this in what now remains of it. This city continued subject to the Mogul government until the period of its decline, when it experienced many of the vicissitudes common to conquered provinces. About the middle of the eighteenth century the province of Agra was ravaged by the Persian despot Ahmed Shah Abdalli, who ordered a general massacre of the wretched people of Mathura. He took the city by storm, and giving it up to plunder, put the inhabitants to the sword for having dared to defend their lives and property. Towards the close of the last century, the province of Agra fell into the hands of the Mahratta conqueror Mahadajee Scindia, and was, in 1803, rescued from his successor Dowlut Rao by Lord Lake.

* A dried raisin.

From Mathura we proceeded towards the capital of the province. On the road the distances are regularly marked by coss stones, the coss being two miles. These stones form large octagonal pillars, from twenty to thirty feet high; they are generally composed of brick and covered with a dark stucco, on which the distances are legibly cut in large characters. The whole of the country from Delhi to Agra is rich in architectural remains, impressing upon the mind of the traveller a grand idea of bygone generations. But it is not abundant only in the noble ruins of past ages; there are also mighty evidences of the taste and capacity of modern times to challenge our admiration and provoke our praise.

From Agra we crossed the Jumna, and proceeded by the usual route to Futtygur. Here we were most hospitably entertained for several days by the commanding officer of a small detachment stationed in this town, which is one of the several military depots on the Ganges. During our stay we witnessed the awful effects of superstition on the human mind, when not counteracted by the higher energies of reason.

About three weeks before our arrival a servant of our host had, by accident, run against an old woman in the bazaar and nearly knocked her down, upon which she poured upon him such a torrent of abuse as to rouse his anger. In a moment of irritation he pushed her violently forward; she immediately fell, and her head came in contact with the stone steps of a house, which cut it severely, and she was picked up senseless. The poor fellow instantly relented, and became dreadfully alarmed at the possible issue of his intemperance. After a short time the woman recovered, but perceiving the person near her who had been the cause of her injury, she caught in her hand the blood which was streaming from her temples, cast it at him with ferocious vehemence, imprecating upon him at the same time the most dreadful maledictions. He remained silent as if paralysed with horror. "May thy shadow grow less and less until it ceases to darken thy path!" cried the sibyl with a half-suppressed scream of rage. "May thy pillow deny thee slumber, and thy food fail to nourish thee! May thy thoughts be curses to thee, and thy heart a plant of bitterness within thee! Before the waning of another moon the alligator shall carouse upon thy devoted body. Thy bones shall never crumble upon the pyre, but rot in infamy. Go, go! thou art accursed—thou bearest an injured woman's malediction!" The man shrank in dismay from the bitter anathema. He returned to his master as a creature under ban and for whom there remained no hope. He could not be persuaded but that the curse pronounced against him was to be his doom. He heard only a prophetic judgment in that horrible denunciation. Deaf to all persuasion, he took little or no food, but gradually declined, and on the day after our arrival at Futtygur, I saw him. He was dejected and low, declaring that his days were numbered, and that his life would terminate before the lapse of forty-eight hours. From this time he tasted no food, or not enough to sustain life, and on the morning of the twenty-eighth day after his adventure in the bazaar, he died.

Similar instances of superstitious belief acting fatally are not uncommon in India, and Colonel Tod, in his "Annals of Rajasthan," mentions a circumstance of this kind so remarkable that I shall offer no apology for inserting it here. Oodi Sing, known from his extreme obesity by the name of the fat Rajah, had fallen in love with the virgin daughter of a Brahmin.

"It was on the Rajah's return from court to his native land that he beheld the damsel, and determined, notwithstanding the sacred function of her father and his own obligations as the dispenser of law and justice, to obtain the object of his admiration. The Brahmin was an Aya Punta, or votary of Aya Mata, whose shrine is at Bai Bhilara. The sectarians of Maroo, very different from the abstinent Brahmins of Bengal, eat flesh, drink wine, and share in all the common enjoyments of life with the martial spirits around them. Whether the scruples of the daughter were likely to be overcome by the royal tempter, or whether the Rajah threatened force, the memoir does not inform us; but as there was no other course by which the father could save her from pollution but by death, he resolved to make it one of vengeance and horror. He dug a sacrificial pit, and having slain his daughter, cut her into fragments and mingled them with pieces of flesh from his own person, made the burnt sacrifice of Aya Mata, and, as the smoke and flames ascended, he pronounced an imprecation on the Rajah. 'Let peace be a stranger to him, and in three pahars,* three days, and three years, let me have my revenge!' Then exclaiming, 'my future dwelling is the Dabi Baori,' sprang into the flaming pit. The horrid tale was related to the Rajah, whose imagination was so haunted by the shade of the Brahmin, that he expired just at the assigned period, a prey to unceasing remorse."

* Hours.

CHAPTER XI.

ANECDOTE OF A HINDOO.—THE NEWAUB OF LUCKNOW.

From Futtygur we crossed the Ganges, and proceeded to Lucknow on the river Goomty. As soon as we reached this splendid metropolis, our palankeen bearers came in a body to congratulate us on our safe arrival at the great city, and at the same time begged we would give them something for having conducted us in safety thus far. We accordingly bought them a sheep, which they soon killed, and converting the flesh into curries regaled themselves, as it appeared, to their infinite satisfaction. They were all Hindoos of the Sudra caste, which is the lowest of the four legitimate divisions. Now, although according to their Vedas and Puranas, even this caste is prohibited from taking the life of animals, except in sacrifice, yet it is certain that while some sects adhere, as the Bhuddists to the letter of the prohibition, even to the preservation of vermin, yet are there a vast number of high caste Hindoos, and even of Brahmins, who do not hesitate to destroy animal life upon particular occasions, though they chiefly confine themselves to animals noxious or wild, except in cases, as above stated, where the love of good feeding induces them to eat as well as to kill. But whilst, however, they will relax on certain points—and where is the community so morally organized that some of its members will not?—they are equally tenacious of their observances upon others, to which they will often adhere even unto death.

At Bombay, I knew an instance of a Hindoo who had gone on board an Indiaman on commercial business, and having taken too strong a dose of opium, he was overcome with drowsiness and fell asleep in the steerage. When he awoke he found that the ship had weighed anchor, and was already several leagues from the fort. There were many Lascars * on board, but, as they were all of inferior caste to himself, the provisions which they had procured for the voyage were looked upon by him as polluted. The captain of the ship, to whom the prejudices of a Hindoo were matters of indifference, refused to send a boat on shore, alleging that it would cause considerable delay. The poor fellow therefore had no alternative but to proceed to Madras with the ship, leaving his family in utter ignorance of what had become of him. On hearing the captain's cruel determination, he lay down upon the deck sullen and dogged, neither moving nor speaking, and in this state he continued for two days without tasting a morsel of food, or once moistening his parched lips. The ship was now at least a hundred leagues from Bombay, though, as she was bound for Madras, she did not keep very far from the land, but coasted down towards Cape Comorin, under easy sail, and was on the morning of the third day about twenty leagues from the shore.

* Native sailors.

By this time the poor Hindoo, overcome with horror at the idea of perishing among a race of beings degraded in his eyes by every moral and personal pollution, requested the captain to allow him a spar upon which he might endeavour to float himself to the nearest point of land, which, as far as I recollect, was Mangalore. It was at least fifty miles distant. A thick spar was accordingly flung into the sea, the Hindoo gallantly plunged in, and, bestriding it, committed himself to the mercy of the calm waters, surrounded by sharks and a host of other perils. Whether the unhappy fanatic reached the shore alive was never ascertained, but the chances were greatly against him.

The devotion of these people is extraordinary, and their capability of endurance incredible. With slight frames, and even when labouring under great bodily debility, they will undergo privations which would destroy the life of a European of much stronger proportions and constitution, while they appear to suffer little or nothing. The chief cause of this may, perhaps, be found in the extreme abstemiousness of their living, which renders them so little liable to inflammatory affections of any kind, that in every part of India even the severest wounds heal in an inconceivably short time with the simple application of a plaister and bandage. I once saw a man in the Deckan at work, six days after he had received a severe fracture of the skull. Owing to his lowness of habit, no inflammation, or to a very trifling extent, ensued.

We reached Lucknow just as the Newaub was

passing down the Goomty in his state barge, the Moah Punkee, of which a faithful representation is given in the following page. It was a splendid sight. This boat derives its name from the figure ornamenting the bow, which is a flying peacock; moah signifies a peacock, and punkee wings, indicating the swiftness of its progress; and these boats certainly are remarkable for their speed. They are of an elegant shape, extremely long and light in form. Unlike every other description of boat, the head rises greatly above the stern, which latter terminates in a low point without the slightest ornament. The head of the boat projects forward with a slight curve, and is at least ten feet from the surface of the water, ending in the body of a peacock with the wings extended. Near this gay ornament is a pavilion sufficiently spacious to contain ten or twelve persons. The boat is manned with from twenty to forty rowers, who use short elliptical paddles, with which they propel her forward with amazing swiftness, timing their strokes by a measured but not unmusical chant. Near the pavilion is a raised platform, upon which a man dances for the amusement of the company, flourishing the while a chowry over his head. He acts as a sort of fugleman, for by his movements the action of the paddles is governed. In the middle ground of the picture appears the palace of Lucknow, which is a structure of much beauty. This celebrated city is situated on the southern bank of the river Goomty, which rises among the Kumaoon hills, whence it flows nearly parallel with the Goggra, and after passing Lucknow and Juanpoor, debouches into the

Ganges, a few miles below Benares. It is called Goomty from its serpentine course; and there are many smaller rivers flowing through the Gangetic plain which have the same name and for the same reason.

As in all the large cities of Hindostan, the greater part of the streets in Lucknow are so narrow as barely to admit the passage of an elephant, and very filthy. The different palaces of the Newaub, and indeed most of the public buildings, are structures of considerable splendour. The Imaum Barrah, completed in the year 1784 by Asoph ud Dowlah, is considered inferior only to the edifices erected by the Mahomedan emperors. The architecture is loaded, though not crowded, with ornament. This building contains a single room a hundred and sixty-seven feet long and broad in proportion. There is one remarkable feature in this structure: no wood has been employed in its erection, it being built entirely of brick. During the Presidency of Mr. Hastings, Lucknow was, perhaps, next to Benares, the richest and most populous city of Hindostan.

A few days after our arrival, together with other English residents, at Lucknow, we received from the Newaub, who was very rich and as hospitable as he was wealthy, an invitation to a sort of public breakfast; after which we were to be regaled by the sight of several novel contests between some of the strongest elephants in the prince's stables. About ten o'clock we accordingly repaired to the palace, where a sumptuous entertainment was provided. It was laid out with Oriental magnificence in a large room with a

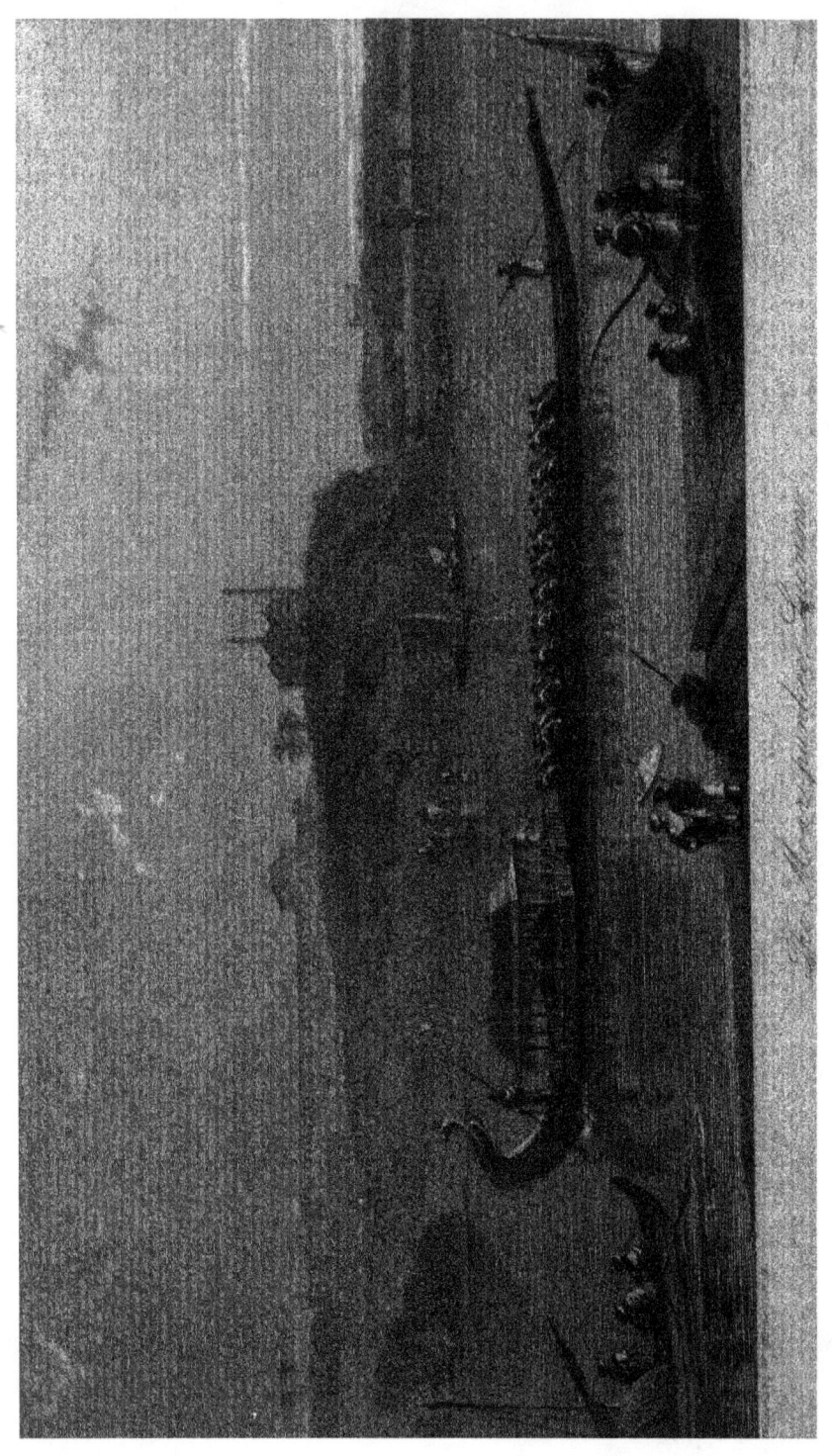

gilded roof. This splendid apartment looked out, through verandas that flanked it on either side, into a spacious area surrounded by trees planted at near intervals, the whole being again encircled by a strong palisade of bamboo.

The splendour of the entertainment sufficiently confirmed what we had heard of the princely hospitality of the Newaub. He received us very graciously, and after having done full justice to his sumptuous provision, we all repaired to the veranda to see a specimen of those elephant fights for which Lucknow has been long celebrated. They were announced as about to commence by three strokes given at unequal intervals on a gong, in order to distinguish this signal from the regular striking of the hour. We had scarcely placed ourselves in such a situation as afforded us the most commanding view of the arena, when a female elephant, followed by two horsemen well mounted and armed with long spears, was conducted into the enclosure. As soon as she reached the centre she looked about her with an apparent complacency that seemed to express a consciousness of the scene which was about to follow; and to my fancy there was a sort of smiling glance occasionally cast from her small twinkling eye, though every other part of her countenance was as rigid as a piece of unpolished horn. She stood all but motionless, merely now and then flapping her ears and slightly twisting her trunk, when two enormous male elephants were admitted by different entrances, and, upon seeing the female, both proceeded briskly towards her; but as soon as each perceived that he had a rival, there was a mutual pause of some duration.

> These were indeed the proud exulting monarchs
> Of the huge herd; their mighty roar invites
> Grateful their willing mates; down their broad cheeks
> The viscid fluid sheds such cooling odour,
> As from the newly ripe kadamba breathes.
> They rend away the lotus leaf and stem
> And roots and filaments, as in the lake
> They madly plunge, affrighting from their nests
> The osprey and the saras,* and to the tune
> Of their ferocious loves, their ponderous ears
> Waved dancing, lash the water into foam.†

It was evident that neither was desirous of commencing hostilities, for each stood alternately looking at the female and at his rival, fearful and undetermined. The men on horseback were already preparing with their long spears, to urge them on to the attack, when one of the huge champions, more resolute than his adversary, advanced towards the female, still with great caution, evidently by no means anxious to begin the encounter, though desirous of inviting her companionship without the intervention of a rival. This was a thing not to be quietly endured; the other elephant, therefore, eyeing him suspiciously, bent forward with the same slow movement, following him step by step. There was now a prospect of immediate collision, and the eyes of the spectators were fixed upon the objects of their eager curiosity. As the two unwieldy combatants had gradually approached

* The Indian crane. † *Hindoo Theatre.*

the subject of contention, they were at length so near to one another that there was no alternative but an immediate conflict. In point of size they were so equally matched that it would have been difficult to determine which had the advantage; and they were said to be about the same age. When within a few yards of each other, the elephant which had got nearest to the female, sprang suddenly forward, with a short abrupt cry, towards his adversary, which having eyed him keenly for some time as if he had expected such a result, was fully prepared for it. The shock was indeed terrific. The tusks of these formidable foes met with a force quite appalling, and the sound of the stroke must have been heard at a considerable distance beyond the enclosure. So fearful was the impetus that both these enormous animals were lifted off their forelegs to the height of at least four feet. Their tusks continued locked for some time without producing mischief, when they gradually retreated, as if by mutual consent. Meanwhile the female appeared to be a perfectly indifferent spectator of the contest. She scarcely deigned to look at the competitors, which were so earnestly contending for the preference in her approbation. It was doubtful whether they had yet relinquished the strife, as both still approached the object of their rivalship, though evidently showing no very vivid anxiety to renew the encounter. There was now a sort of tacit menacing kept up between them, until the two horsemen galloped forward from behind and began to goad them in the flanks in order to induce them to renew hostilities. This summary proceeding, instead of increasing their irritation towards each other, provoked their rage against the horsemen, upon whom both instantly turned, and pursued them with a speed that bid fair to render fruitless the utmost efforts of their horses. I confess I expected every moment to see one of the riders seized by the trunk of the excited elephant and either whirled into the air or crushed to death under the weight of its ponderous body, but by the dexterity of his horsemanship and the superior speed of his horse, he managed to escape, although at one time he was in no little jeopardy.

The elephants were now led from the enclosure, and others introduced, when the same scene was almost precisely repeated, until the amusement began to lose its interest and to grow exceedingly tiresome. After the first shock the combatants invariably declined to try a second, which I could not help thinking a most prudent determination. A tusk of one of them was broken off close to the jaw, and the animal led from the arena streaming with blood. The unfortunate creature was most probably rendered useless by this accident, as the tusk when broken almost invariably becomes diseased; the wound constantly suppurating renders the animal unable to perform its customary services. We at length became completely weary of the sport, and retired with the good wishes of the Newaub, who seemed pleased at the idea that he had availed himself of the opportunity of entertaining us. The elephants at Lucknow have been long celebrated for their prowess in these encounters; but I must own that on witnessing them I was greatly disappointed.

A few days after, we received another invitation from the Newaub to witness a fight between an elephant and an alligator; this we willingly accepted, expecting to see something tremendous from the collision of two animals so formidable and so different in their habits and character. His highness had made the necessary preparations for affording us this new species of entertainment, having sent to the river Goggra a party, who had succeeded in catching a couple of large alligators, one of which was seven-and-twenty feet long. They were conveyed from the banks of the Goggra to the Goomty upon hackeries.

On reaching the scene intended for this strange sport, we found the alligators so exhausted from the uncongenial mode of their conveyance, and from having been so long without food, that they could scarcely crawl, but remained upon the banks of the stream without attempting to escape, and in a state of almost complete inaction. One, however, was much more torpid than the other, in consequence of having been longer caught and consequently longer a sufferer. A large elephant was at length led to the spot, though it approached with evident symptoms of distrust; for these animals appear to have an instinctive perception of danger far more keen than any other beast of the forest. He eyed the hideous monster which lay half gasping upon the river bank, for several moments before he ventured to advance, and when at length he did so, the largest alligator opened its ponderous jaws and made a snap at his trunk, but he had taken care to curl it up between his tusks, thus securing it from injury. The alligator finding itself foiled, snapped at its aggressor's legs, but as the effort was made without any vigour or quickness, the elephant easily evaded the intended infliction by actively retreating beyond the reach of its dreadful fangs. Carefully avoiding a nearer approach to an enemy who it was evident had still the power to do him a serious mischief, he cautiously advanced towards the other alligator which was lying on the bank in an almost exhausted state, and on getting close to it, coiled up his trunk as before that it might be beyond the reach of harm, then placing his foot upon the body of the huge reptile, pressed upon it with the whole weight of his own. The creature immediately opened its mouth to a hideous extent and gave a shrill scream; but though crushed by such a weight, it was so tenacious of life, that it was not dead when we left the ground, and revived considerably upon water being thrown over it. The gnashing of the monster's jaws, when the elephant trod upon it, might I should think have been heard at a distance of at least two hundred yards.

A pariah dog was now fastened by a strong cord to this alligator, which immediately took him into its mouth, but to our utter astonishment the dog soon released himself from his horrible prison, and attacking the animal's nose, bit it so severely that the blood copiously flowed. The creature seemed to be quite insensible of the infliction, and was manifestly so nearly exhausted as to be almost bereft of sensation. To this circumstance must of course be attributed the dog's escape from his perilous confinement. His head, however, was more than once within the alligator's mouth, but he seemed to thrust it in with impunity, and to draw it out at pleasure. Having at length seized his dying enemy again by the nose, he bit it with such severity that the alligator, as if in its expiring agony, opened its jaws and immediately closing them upon its tormentor, crushed him so forcibly that when he was extracted, which was immediately done by one of the attendants who was present to conduct the sports, he appeared to be quite dead. Water was again thrown upon the alligator and the dog. Upon the former it had little or no effect; but the latter, to our extreme surprise, almost immediately rose up, staggered for a few seconds, and then, the moment it was released, ran off as if nothing had happened.

The Newaub had a space of ground of several acres enclosed, within which he kept a large assortment of birds and beasts of prey. It was a very fine collection. Amongst a great variety of animals there were several couples of the Rhamghur hill dogs, which go in packs to the number of several hundred, hunting down and quickly despatching the most ferocious tiger. They were animated creatures, but did not appear to be particularly fierce. Their size was about that of a stag-hound. They were kept in cages, for they are not easily domesticated, their wild nature taking them continually into the jungles in search of game. They often run down a whole herd of deer and leave not one alive.

CHAPTER XII.

A MAUSOLEUM.—ASOPH UD DOWLAH.

Among the architectural objects worthy of notice at Lucknow, is a mausoleum erected to the memory of a female relative of Newaub Asoph ud Dowlah. It is placed in a garden with a terraced walk and fountains. The building in the distance, as represented in the picture, is a private mosque, built by the immediate predecessor of that prince by whom we were so hospitably entertained. The garden is spacious, and laid out with much taste. The principal building stands upon a square platform, which is ascended by four or five steps, and forms a terrace of considerable width. The tomb is an octagon terminating in a richly ornamented parapet with short minarets at each angle. A large dome rises from the centre of the roof surmounted by a lofty gilt culice. The pediment beneath the parapet projects from the wall about three feet, giving a graceful finish to the body of the building.

At a little distance it is difficult to say whether the mausoleum is not constructed of the finest marble, but a closer inspection shows that it is covered with chunam only, a composition which for a long period preserves its pure white surface uninjured.

It is astonishing to what a degree of perfection the natives of India carry the art of stuccoing with this beautiful material, producing an effect so near to that of white marble, that it often requires a close scrutiny to detect the imitation. As neither frost, nor snow, nor any of the sudden atmospheric changes, to which most other countries are subject, occur in this "land of the sun," the chunam resists even those awful storms with which every region between the tropics is more or less visited at certain periods of the year, and will last for generations without showing the slightest symptoms of decay.

The mosque in the distance, though simple, is not devoid of elegance, which is much enhanced by the two lofty minarets that ornament the transverse angles of the square.

The body of Asoph ud Dowlah, who built the mausoleum just described, is buried in a sepulchre constantly illuminated by an immense number of wax tapers. The sarcophagus in which his body reposes, is continually strewed with flowers and strips of gilt paper; why the latter, I never heard explained. The tomb is kept covered with consecrated bread from the city of the Prophet, whence a supply at certain intervals is obtained at an enormous expense, and passages from the Koran are chanted day and night over the mouldering ashes of the prince. A censer filled with various perfumes is placed on one side of the sepulchre, and his sword and cummerbund on the other. At the head a copy of the Koran and his turban are deposited.

Lucknow is about six hundred and fifty miles from Calcutta, and is consequently visited by many residents at the Presidency, especially by ladies as anxious to see the elephant fights and other novelties for which this city is celebrated, as they of the nobler gender, who deem the enjoyment of such stern amusements their especial privilege.

A very interesting circumstance connected with Lucknow occurred about three years ago, to the recital of which I shall devote the remainder of this short chapter.

Some thirty years since, the captain of an Indiaman residing in this city, obtained an introduction to a Persian lady of great personal attractions, of whom he shortly after became enamoured. She returned his affections and they married. The lady being in possession of great wealth, the husband relinquished his profession and took up his permanent abode at Lucknow. Here he resided with his wife for upwards of three years in great domestic comfort, during which period she bore him three children. From this time he was absent until the eldest boy was about seven years of age, when the father brought him to England in order to obtain for him the advantages of a European education. It happened that the quondam captain, for some reason now only to be surmised, led his child to suppose that he was not related to him but merely a friend to whose care he had been committed during the voyage. Almost immediately upon their arrival in this country, the father suddenly died without revealing to his charge

the relationship subsisting between them. As the boy bore the complexion of his native clime, and the features of the race from which he sprang on the maternal side, he was looked upon as a half-caste by the relatives of the deceased, who had never been informed of the father's marriage; they, therefore, considered that they made a suitable provision for him by binding him an apprentice to a grocer, with whom he served his time and proved a faithful and assiduous servant. When the period of his apprenticeship was completed, the relations of his late father gave him a hundred pounds and cast him upon the wide world to seek his fortune, at the same time discouraging any expectation of future assistance; glad to be thus easily freed from the claims of one whom they deemed an incumbrance.

Without patron or friend, the deserted youth had little chance of establishing himself in his business by securing a respectable connexion—a half-caste being looked upon with a kind of conventional prejudice, which it is to be hoped the late act of Parliament in favour of this slighted race will tend speedily to subdue. Thus circumstanced, he was at length reduced to such a state of destitution that, in order to prevent the accession of irremediable poverty, he became an itinerant dealer in tea, and in this humble capacity contrived to realize an uncertain subsistence, which he rendered still more precarious by adding to his domestic responsibilities that expensive blessing—a wife. He married the daughter of a labouring carpenter, with whom he casually became acquainted, dexterity. She was a comely woman, and, fortunately for him, turned out an excellent manager; his expenses were therefore not materially increased.

Having been represented to the servants of a gentleman residing in the country as an honest fellow who sold excellent tea for a small profit, he found among them a ready sale for the commodity in which he dealt; and though they were keen chafferers and generally pushed a hard bargain with him, still he was constant in his attendance upon them, as the establishment was large, the sale therefore considerable, and his money returns quick. His civility moreover was appreciated, so that he always found a ready welcome among those merry domestics.

He was one day upon the point of quitting the house, when he chanced to pass the master as the latter was ascending the steps of the portico. The gentleman seemed suddenly struck with his appearance, eyeing him with an eager and somewhat impatient curiosity. The poor huckster, for he occasionally sold other things besides tea when he found he could turn such traffic to profitable account, felt abashed at the rigid and unexpected scrutiny, touched his hat with a tremulous obsequiousness as he passed the lord of the mansion, and made the best of his way home, fearing that the gentleman had entertained some unfavourable suspicion of him. As soon as he had retired, the master asked his servants what they knew respecting him, and though this was very little, it was still sufficient to induce him to desire again to see the itinerant tea-dealer; he therefore gave orders that he should be apprised the next time the latter called.

This was accordingly done, and when the poor fellow was introduced to the great man, he began to entertain fears that he was labouring under the odium of a base suspicion. The old gentleman commenced by questioning him about his birth and parentage. His replies at length convinced the inquirer that the humble vender of tea was the object for whom he had been some time in search.

It happened that this very gentleman was residing at Lucknow at the time of the captain's marriage with the Persian lady, and was in fact the only European, besides her husband, with whom she had been acquainted. He was moreover present at the marriage, and the sole attesting witness. The widow had latterly written him several earnest letters from Lucknow, imploring him to use his best endeavours to recover her boy, of whom she had heard nothing for nearly twenty years. Upon receiving an appeal so urgent and affecting, the kind-hearted friend did his best to discover the lost son, but having no clue and finding his efforts end in disappointment, he had abandoned all hopes of success, when the resemblance of the huckster to the Indian lad, as the former quitted his house on the morning of the preceding day, struck him so forcibly, that he felt instantly convinced of their identity, which his subsequent enquiries confirmed.

The old gentleman now made the long-neglected half-caste, as he was considered to be, acquainted with every particular of his birth, informing him that the person who brought him to England was his father, and that he had a mother in India who was longing to clasp him to her bosom. She had deposited several thousand pounds in the Calcutta bank for his use should he be discovered, and was inconsolable at his mysterious absence. Her affection never for a moment subsided: she had mourned for him as for one dead, though not without a hope of still meeting him, in spite of her long and bitter disappointment.

This intelligence came like a light from heaven upon the friendless outcast. He could for the moment scarcely believe so flattering a reality; but it was indeed true that he who had for years been reduced to the hard necessity of trudging about the country with a hawker's licence, abandoned by those relatives who should have protected him from such degradation, was destined to come into the possession of great wealth, which his former privations have taught him how to enjoy. His newly discovered friend furnished him with immediate letters to his agent in Calcutta. He secured a passage without delay, and after a prosperous voyage, reached the City of Palaces, whither his mother quickly repaired, with a large retinue, to receive and convey him to her own magnificent abode at Lucknow. Shortly after his arrival he sent to England for his wife, who followed in the first ship that sailed after the receipt of his letter. These latter transactions took place within the last three years. The parties are now at Lucknow, living in splendour and happiness. These few simple facts might furnish the groundwork of a romance of no ordinary interest. Their authenticity may be relied on.

CHAPTER XIII.

THE RAJPOOTNI BRIDE.

Scarcely a day passed, during our stay at this splendid city, without something or other of novelty occurring to afford us entertainment. The Newaub's menagerie was a scene of frequent resort, but especially the palace gardens, which are laid out with great magnificence, and contain several very elegant buildings.

The Newaub had in his service a troop of Rajpoot cavalry, in which there was one of the finest men I ever beheld. He was in the prime of life, in the full vigour of his strength, remarkably expert in all the manly exercises peculiar to his tribe, and as powerful as he was active. He was pointed out to all strangers at Lucknow as a person of extraordinary qualities both of mind and body. He stood about six feet and an inch high, as erect as a column, with a frame, though not heavily muscular, yet knit with a compactness that combined elegance and strength in an unusual degree. The development was not prominent, and though rather of a spare habit, yet the contour of his frame displayed the most graceful anatomical outline, while the firm texture of the muscles showed that they were capable of more, than ordinary exertion. The man was altogether extremely handsome, his nose being small and of perfect symmetry, his lips rather inclining to fulness, and his eyes uncommonly brilliant. He had a delicate curly moustache and but little beard. He was admired by all the women of Lucknow, nor did the men look on him with less admiration, though of a different kind: still he manifested no consciousness of superiority, save in that expression of independence inseparable from his race, and which told that he gloried in the name of Rajpoot. He was the grandson of a Hara chieftain, whose end had been as sanguinary as the cause was tragical. The recital exhibits such a faithful picture of the Rajpoot character, that I offer no excuse for introducing it here.

It happened that a feud had existed for several generations, in the families of two chieftains, a Hara and a Rahtore. Nothing can exceed the animosity which prevails among these stern and uncompromising warriors when such deadly inheritances are left them to maintain. It is next to impossible to effect a reconciliation, and it seldom or never happens but that these unnatural animosities have eventually the most fatal issues. The Hara had a daughter as celebrated for her beauty as for her energy of character and masculine understanding. Though subjected to the rigid discipline and jealous seclusion general among the daughters of Rajpoot princes, she had nevertheless partially emancipated herself from a control so repugnant to her impatient yet resolute temperament, and had not only become a partner in the counsels of her parent, but was consulted by him upon every pressing emergency. Although

She never did apply
Hot and rebellious liquors to her blood,

she was of a fiery and daring spirit, and her father scarcely regretted being without a son, that paramount blessing of all Rajpoot marriages, in having a daughter so pre-eminently possessing the high moral energies of her race.

This extraordinary woman had been sought in marriage by many a bold aspirant, though none of the chiefs in her immediate vicinity had succeeded in securing her affections. Her beauty and vigour of mind were the theme of every tongue.

> Her forehead some fair moon, her brows a bow,
> Love's pointed darts her piercing eye-beams glow;
> Her breath adds fragrance to the morning air;
> At once the lover's hope and his despair;—
> Her teeth pomegranate seeds; her smiles soft lightnings are.
> Her feet like leaves of lotus on the lake
> When with the passing breeze they gently shake;
> Her movements graceful as the swan that laves
> His snowy plumage on the rippling waves.*

It happened that the beautiful Rajpootni was one day hunting in company with her father when a tiger, darting from a thicket, sprang upon her horse and thus put her life in immediate jeopardy. Instead of exhibiting any of the ordinary fears of her sex, she hastily shook her raven locks from her temples, and with her head undauntedly raised, her lips com-

---

* Broughton's translations from the Popular Poetry of the Hindoos.

pressed, and her eye flashing with a wild energy, she resolutely attacked the tiger with a dagger which she carried in her girdle, plunging it up to the very hilt in the animal's body. The excited beast, finding itself thus unexpectedly assailed, and roused to tenfold rage by the wound she had just inflicted upon it, quitted the horse and turned upon the rider. Her danger was imminent, yet she did not quail; on the contrary, her resolution seemed to increase with her peril. It was evident, notwithstanding, that she could not successfully cope with an assailant so fearful, and her father was unfortunately at too great a distance to afford her aid. At this critical moment, when with extended and foaming jaws her ferocious adversary was in the act of seizing her by the head, a young hunter darted forward on his well-conditioned steed with the swiftness of the blast, and as he shot by like a thunderbolt, with a single stroke of his sabre, severed the tiger's head from its body. The gory trunk instantly fell to the ground, leaving the intrepid huntress unscathed. The vanquished brute in its dying agonies, short as they were, fixed its claws in the flanks of the poor horse, and lacerated them so severely that it was found necessary to destroy it on the spot. The lady thus providentially rescued, looked round for her preserver, but he was at a distance urging his horse to its utmost speed; she had, nevertheless, seen sufficient of his features to distinguish that he was a Rahtore; for these Rajpoot tribes have always a something discriminative of their respective clans. This discovery was painful, as it recalled to her mind the feud which her father was maintaining with all that vindictiveness of spirit so frequently and fearfully verified in the Rajpoot chronicles.

The old Hara, who had been sufficiently near to perceive what had happened, approached his child with a gloomy austerity of countenance, to the cause of which she was no stranger. He too had distinguished the Rahtore: his grim silence and the stern composure of his features sufficiently expressed that he had recognized her deliverer. Not a word was exchanged. The Rajpoot did not express, even by a look, his satisfaction at his child's escape, and she with an aspect of calm but haughty indifference, mounted a camel and accompanied her parent home without the interchange of a word. She could not, however, efface from her mind the image of the young Rahtore. His manly bearing, his strength and dexterity, fired her imagination. He was perpetually present in her dreams, and the sole object of her waking thoughts. His fine muscular frame, the clear rapid gleam of his eye, the haughty bend of his brow and animated expansion of nostril, the grace with which he rode, his prowess and skill in the use of the tulwar, or scimitar—all rose to her view in rapid succession, imbued with the colourings of an ardent prepossession, and she determined, at whatever cost, to behold the object which had thus irresistibly entranced her imagination. Her resolution was a bold one, and therefore her unbending soul maintained it with the greater pertinacity.

For some time she failed in all her efforts to obtain a sight of her deliverer. Her father watched her with a scrutiny so unremitting that she could not evade the morbid keenness of his vigilance. She, nevertheless, contrived to employ emissaries, but in vain: they only returned to bring her the unwelcome tidings of their failure. Still disappointment seemed rather to add strength to than weaken her resolution; and notwithstanding the gloom occasionally gathering on her parent's brow, which invariably darkened to a deeper shade whenever an allusion was made to her rescue from the tiger, her determination had abated nothing: her indomitable spirit was of too high a temper to blench, though her perseverance had not been rewarded with success.

At length, as she was again one day hunting with her father in the jungle, emerging from a tangled path into a narrow vista of the wood, she saw at a distance a single horseman pressed by several assailants, who appeared about to overpower him. On a nearer approach she discovered that they were, as she had suspected, part of a dacoit gang attacking a Rahtore chief. She instantly spurred her horse forward and discharged an arrow at the foremost assailant, who received it in his right temple and dropped dead. The robbers fled when they perceived that others were coming to the rescue of their victim. Upon reaching the spot where the encounter between the dacoits and the young Rajpoot had taken place, his fair rescuer found him lying on the ground weltering in his blood, and desperately wounded. He had been cut down by a sabre stroke, and the wound presented a most ominous aspect of fatality. The brave Rajpootni instantly perceived that it was her late deliverer who was lying senseless before her. She did not rend the air with her shrieks, but calmly tore a strip from the turban of one of her attendants, bandaged the wound tightly in order to stanch the blood, then desired that the Rahtore should be lifted into a palankeen, which had fortunately been ordered to await her commands at the skirts of the jungle, and immediately borne to the house of her father. When, on the arrival of the party at the Hara's abode, he was taken from the palankeen, the old warrior discovered that his wounded guest was the head of that clan with whom his family had been so long at strife. Though this was a galling discovery, it did not preclude the generous offices of hospitality. These were rigidly performed, yet the rancour which gnawed at the vitals of the Hara chief did not for one moment abate. Whilst, however, he gave orders that every attention should be paid to the stranger, bitterness and curses were in his heart. " May his shadow diminish," he murmured when there was no one by to catch the echo of his thoughts, " until he stalk a tortured spirit over the scene of his pilgrimage ! May prosperity never spread her wings over his dwelling, but the scourge of desolation smite him and his! Should he become a husband and a parent, may his children be fatherless and his wife a widow!"

These and similar maledictions were continually in his mouth; nevertheless, it did not abate the scrupulousness of his hospitality, and the young Rahtore was tended with the most careful attention, until he was in a condition to be conveyed to his own dwelling. During the short period of his confinement under the roof of his family foe, he had found an opportunity to declare his passion for his lovely preserver. He told her that he had long attempted to smother it, on account of the enmity mutually subsisting between their houses, but had found it impossible to do so. This was neither an unexpected nor unwelcome avowal. His young and beautiful nurse — for the daughter of the Hara chief had anxiously attended upon him — heard him therefore without surprise, but not without pleasure, and before he quitted her parent's roof, their vows of eternal attachment had been reciprocally plighted.

Although his wound had been desperate, he was not long in recovering, and when sufficiently strong to appear abroad, he made overtures to the hereditary foe of his family to bestow the hand of his daughter upon him. The old man was roused to the most ferocious indignation at a proposal which he considered so derogatory to the pride of his house, bound as he was by the stern obligation of hereditary enmity to maintain the feud so long existing between it and that of the Rahtore. He consequently rejected the proposal in terms of the harshest severity, at the same time reproaching the young warrior who had so frankly solicited an alliance with his family, with a breach of honour in having seduced the affections of his child, at a moment too when he was at the point of death under her father's roof, and receiving all the kind offices of a scrupulous hospitality. This accusation was repudiated with the wild indignation and keen sensibility of wrong peculiar to the high-spirited Rajpoot, and not be ungrateful, father; 'tis the vice of contemptible souls."

He saved your life and you have in return saved his; thus the obligations of gratitude are annulled. He was ministered to in his extremity under the roof of his hereditary foe, and sent back unscathed to his own dwelling. Your debt has been fairly cancelled. If there be a balance it is on his side."

"True, father, and he is willing to lay the balance at your feet by making your daughter happy. Remember, when she was in jeopardy, to use the words of our own native bard,*

> The guardian youth appeared
> And, heedless of a person which enshrines
> The worth of all the world, quick interposed
> His powerful arm to snatch me from destruction.
> For me he braved the monster's mighty blows,
> Falling like thunder-strokes.
>   The tiger plied
> His fangs and claws in vain; the hero triumphed—
> The furious savage fell beneath his sword."

"No more of this—you know me, girl; I must hear no more. Would you bring the evil influence upon your father's house? The very stones would cry out in indignation against you. Remember a parent's command is not to be trifled with. I brook not trifling."

She was silent, but the broad steady gleam of her eye told at once that it was not the silence of acquiescence. Her heart rose to her very throat as the Hara retired, and her determination increased in pro-

* Bhavabhuti.

portion as her feelings were suppressed. She from this moment sought an opportunity to burst the bonds of restraint and escape from a tyranny which had become in the highest degree repulsive to her energetic soul. She passed several days in the silence of her chamber, from which she seldom stirred, and the result was a resolution to thwart the tyranny of her parent's vindictive refusal, by flying to the arms of the man in whom she discovered a kindred spirit, and knew every feeling of his heart to be perfectly germane with her own. She accordingly sent him, by a trusty messenger, a picture which represented a hunter rescuing a fawn from the claws of a tiger. He readily understood the allusion and returned to her a communication in a similar hieroglyphical form, exhibiting the same hunter with the fawn nestled in his bosom and a dove flying over it, to denote the speed with which he was preparing to execute her wishes. Several other communications, and of a like kind, passed between the lovers, until there was a mutual understanding as to the course each should pursue.

The father, who had one of those indomitable tempers which is the Hara's boast, though he doated on his child as far as was compatible with his stern nature, had nevertheless treated her with uniform severity ever since she made her declaration of attachment to the Rahtore; still he entertained not the slightest suspicion that she would, under any circumstances, dare to compromise the dignity of his house by such an act of disobedience as she meditated. It was plain that he knew her not. He confided in her inflexible spirit as a safeguard against dishonour. He felt satisfied that she would make any sacrifice, however painful, to support the glory of her race; but amidst all this asperity of feeling, he was proud of her beauty, and it fully justified his pride.

>Mark her slender form bent low,
>As the zephyrs lightly blow!
>Mark her robes like blossoms rare,
>Scattering fragrance on the air!
>Lotus-like her dewy feet
>Treasures yield of nectar'd sweet;
>Lightly as her footsteps pass,
>Blushes* all the bending grass;
>And rings of jewels, beauty's powers,
>Freshen into living flowers,†
>While brighter tints and rosier hues
>All the smiling earth suffuse.‡

* The Hindoo ladies are accustomed to stain the soles of their feet with a crimson dye.

† In the East, ornaments of gold and jewels are often made in the forms of flowers.

‡ Broughton's translations from the Popular Poetry of the Hindoos.

CHAPTER XIV.

THE RAJPOOTNI BRIDE.

One morning the father and daughter were as usual enjoying together the pleasures of the chase, when they were separated as before. A boar having started from a thicket, was instantly pursued by the bold huntress. The animal was large, powerful, and greatly excited by a slight wound which it had received in the shoulder from one of the shikarries, whom it had immediately charged and disabled. The undaunted Rajpootni fearlessly approached the enemy; it instantly turned, struck her horse in the flank, and ploughing up the flesh, laid the ribs bare. She, however, delivered her spear with unerring precision, forcing it through the boar's body;—the savage beast rolled upon the plain and expired. This was a deed of prowess that would have done honour to any masculine arm. Whilst she was breathing her wounded steed after this rough encounter, a horseman suddenly emerged from the thicket, came up to the fair vanquisher, dismounted, placed her upon his own fiery courser, sprang up before her, then, pressing his heels against the sides of his faithful Arab, plunged into the jungle in the sight of her father and his numerous attendants. It was the Rahtore; there was no mis-

taking him. Vain was pursuit, for the fugitives were at a distance, and soon disappeared amid the thick recesses of the forest.

The venerable Hara returned from the chase imprecating curses on his child, and vowing the most deadly vengeance against her audacious paramour. The lovers, when they thought themselves beyond the reach of pursuit, slackened their speed and proceeded leisurely towards the Rahtore's abode. Immediately upon his return, the bereaved father summoned his followers to avenge the abduction of his daughter. His faithful Rajpoots were ready at his call, and upwards of three hundred men stood before him to rescue his child and inflict a signal punishment upon her ravisher. The old man prepared to march with the dawn, every dark passion of his soul boiling like a lava-flood within him. All those feelings which a fierce sense of injury now wrung from his unrelenting nature, were concentrated into one absorbing impulse of revenge. He had no energy but for hatred and vengeance, and the sullen calmness with which he prepared to execute their ruthless injunctions, at once betrayed the intensity of his savage purpose. With the full blight of his passions upon him, he proceeded to the temple of his divinity, and laid his propitiatory sacrifice upon the unhallowed altar. It was an oblation too sanguinary to be accepted by a just and merciful God:—the smoke of his incense ascended not beyond the gorgeous dome of the desecrated sanctuary. The officiating Brahmin, however, as the vicarious minister of the deity to whom the sacrifice was presented, accepted the suppliant's offering, giving him assurance of success, upon which the spiritual tribute was doubled. The unholy worshipper then quitted the presence of the divinity to whom he had been taught thus to exhibit his demoniacal homage, with the confidence of a divine sanction for any act of desperate retribution he might commit.

The morning broke brightly upon the slumbers of the indignant father; he awoke with the heavens smiling above and around him, but with a hell burning in his heart. Mounting his charger, he proceeded in silence at the head of his followers towards the abode of his hereditary foe. His impatience of revenge rendered the journey long and distasteful. A raven perched upon a tree on the roadside as he passed, presented an unfavourable omen; nevertheless, assured by the promises of the Brahmin, he interpreted it in his own favour and to the prejudice of him by whom he had been so grievously wronged. His soul was parched with a thirst which nothing but the blood of his enemy could appease. Halting his little troop after sunset under a large grove of trees, he ordered them to refresh themselves with food and rest and waited impatiently for the dawn. The night was calm, but deepened by the shadows of the surrounding groves. The scene " suited the gloomy habit of his soul," which was as sombre as the prospect immediately around him. Nature at length gave way, and, even under the inflictions of his own fierce passions, he slept. The moon rose, and traversed the blue plains of heaven like a fair angel of light, heralded by stars and embracing in her retinue the glories of a universe;

while the wretched mortal who lay slumbering beneath the influence of her gentle effulgence saw nothing but the gloom within—was awake to nothing but the darkness of his own blighted spirit.

Meanwhile, at the Rahtore's dwelling all was harmony and rejoicing. The bridal feast was prepared; the bride and bridegroom had ratified the compact to which their hearts had been mutually pledged. They looked abroad into the clear calm sky, and hailed the celestial presence which seemed, to their glowing fancies, to smile upon their union. Their hearts were buoyant; the sounds of mirth and congratulation were in their ears. The neighbours had assembled: the tomtom,* the sittar,† the sarinda,‡ the kurtaul,§ the saringee,|| were uniting their harmonies in order to animate the guests. The voice of joy was in the feast, when it was interrupted by intelligence that the Hara chief was approaching to avenge the rape of his daughter. The banquet was abruptly suspended, and without a moment's delay the Rahtore mustered his followers. These were few, but resolute; they did not amount to more than a hundred and fifty men: nevertheless, their brave leader shrank not from the encounter, as a true Rajpoot never declines a contest, whatever the odds against him;—with him death is always preferable to disgrace.

The young bridegroom did not give the enemy time to take him by surprise, but, sallying forth, accompanied by his small yet determined band, resolved to fight to the last in defence of his honour and of his

---

* Drum. † Guitar. ‡ Violin. § Cymbals.
|| An instrument played at weddings.

wife, who cheered him on his departure, bidding him a prosperous issue, and adding, that she should have the pile prepared in case of his defeat. She gave him her parting benediction, and said, with subdued emotion " Should thy discomfiture be the decree of the Eternal, thy soul shall not occupy the swerga-bowers alone — thy sita* will accompany thee to the abodes of the brave." He departed with the most deadly resolves. The adverse parties met; the encounter was tremendous: there was no shrinking, neither mercy felt nor quarter given — revenge was the cry and death the issue. The weight of numbers was on the side of the Hara, but the advantage of prowess on that of the Rahtore; still nothing could withstand such fearful odds as two to one, especially where both sides were proverbially brave. The bereaved father, panting for vengeance, sought his adversary through the thickest of the fight, and at length they met. There was a deadly deliberation in the aspect of both, and the conflict was proportionably stubborn; but the declining strength of age was no match for the undiminished vigour of youth. The Hara was struck down by a blow from his adversary's sabre; fortunately, his quilted tunic resisted the stroke sufficiently to protect his body from a fatal incision. The Rahtore, when he saw his foe prostrate before him, remembering that he was the father of his bride, forbore to repeat the blow. Quitting his vanquished enemy, he plunged into the thickest of the fight, where his sword did signal execution; but his numbers momentarily diminished. It was clear that

* Sita signifies spouse.

they must be finally overpowered; yet they maintained the unequal contest with unflinching constancy.

A hundred and eighty of the enemy had fallen; they nevertheless still retained an overwhelming majority. Upwards of a hundred Rahtores were lying on the field of slaughter, but the fury of the fight did not slacken. The field was strewed with dead, and the survivors were every moment adding to the number of the slain. The Hara chief performed acts of valour which would not have disgraced his best days; but his thirst of revenge was unslaked while he saw his valiant foe alive. He encountered him a second time, and defeat was again the result. At length, after a desperate struggle, the Rahtores were cut off to a man; their leader alone escaped alive, and he quitted the field under the cover of evening, leaving but fifty of his enemies to tell the story of their sanguinary victory.

The brave though vanquished chief retired, weary and dispirited, into the neighbouring forest. He was goaded by remorse at the idea of having survived a contest in which all his companions had obtained the soldier's noblest meed—a glorious death on the field of battle, whilst he was skulking into the covert, under the veil of darkness, like a hunted beast of prey, as if to avoid a foe from whom death would now be a boon. At first his thoughts were so many goads that irritated, to an insupportable degree, the lacerations of his fiery spirit, but, in proportion as these paroxysms gave way to calm reflection, he seemed to rise above his condition and to be endued with new energies. He felt his soul on a sudden expand with the contemplation of some mighty enterprise, and while every nerve within his quivering frame seemed newly strung, he uttered, in the vehemence of his excited feelings, a deep, hoarse vow of vengeance. At this moment a lion crossed his path in the clear moonlight. It appeared to be ominous of his future destiny. "Now," thought he, "here is the representative of my deadliest enemy. I will attack the monster with my sword, and, if I destroy him, it will be the pledge of my future revenge on the man to whom I owe a death. If I perish in the encounter, it will be a fortunate release at once from misery and disgrace."

He was armed with a conical shield which was strengthened by a thick brass boss, projecting from the centre, and terminating in a blunt point. Raising his heavy tulwar, he undauntedly approached the lion, which had by this time manifested symptoms of hostility so fearfully indicative of its deadly intentions. Its head was slightly depressed: its eyes glared with appalling ferocity: it licked its quivering chaps, opening every now and then its vast mouth as if to show the formidable weapons with which its jaws were armed. The Rahtore, nothing dismayed by these preliminary menaces, approached the grim savage with a quick step, dashed his shield violently against its head, and struck it so vigorous a blow across the skull as to cleave it in twain. The beast fell instantly dead before him. He smiled savagely as he saw it extended at his feet, as impotent to harm him as the earth-worm above which it lay.

Returning pensively from the spot, he approached his home with a sad and ominous presentiment. He dreaded to encounter the reproaches of his bride, who, he knew, would not think favourably of his escape from a field which had terminated so disastrously for him. There was a weight upon his spirits which he could not shake off, but, trusting to the strength of her young affections, he bent forward with some confidence to meet her. When he reached the house which during the previous day had resounded with the bridal festivity, he found the door barred, and was thus denied an entrance to his home. Thinking that this might have been done in order to prevent surprise from the enemy, he knocked with a determined but trembling hand. He who had fearlessly braved death in its most appalling forms, cowered before the anticipated indignation of a woman. As the door was not opened, he struck upon it with the hilt of his scimitar.

" Who knocks ?" calmly asked a voice from within, which he instantly recognised, and his heart thrilled with the tenderest emotions.

" Thy bridegroom, my sita," he replied with the energy of awakened passion; " open, and bid him welcome."

"Hah! how went the battle?" inquired the Rajpootni in the same unimpassioned but somewhat stern tone, that sent a cold chill through the whole mass of his blood.

"Against us. I alone am left to tell the sad tale of defeat. Every Rahtore, save myself, lies upon the bloody field. It was in truth a contest of extermination. Seeing that all was lost, I saved a worthless life for thy sake. Open, love."

"To whom?"

"Thy husband."

"I have none. He perished on the bloody field from which thou hast ignobly fled. He never would have returned but with victory on his brow."

"Dost thou deny me, sita?—thy bridegroom of yesterday—thy champion for ever!"

"He who called me bride, has taken his draught of the amreeta-cup.* He was no recreant to retire from the field of glory and leave the sable garland of death upon every head but his own. He never would have saved an inglorious life to skulk through the world with the brand of infamy upon him. My husband was no coward. Thou art a stranger to this desolate bosom. Go from the door of the widow-bride who knows the sacrifice due to one who is dead to her for ever."

The Rahtore was deeply stung with the reproof. It fell like a blight upon his heart. He felt the full force of her calm but haughty interdiction, and quailed beneath that heroism which abashed his own. He was repudiated by her who was the magnet to which all his affections clung with a tenacity that even her scorn could not subdue. She stigmatized him with the name of coward; she refused him admittance to her presence; she denied that he any longer retained an influence over her affections; she scorned, she rejected him. She had talked of a sacrifice, and the most fearful apprehensions began to take possession of

* The cup of immortality.

his mind. He knew her resolved energy of purpose, her uncompromising notions of honour, her recklessness of suffering, her high sense of conjugal obligations, and her scrupulosity in adhering to the most rigid observances which custom had, as it were, sanctified among the caste of which it was her pride to be a member. Dreading the fearful import of her words, and knowing the austere bent of her determination, he struck again fiercely on the door with his shield, at the same time entreating, in a tone of the most pathetic persuasion, that she would immediately admit him. She did not condescend to reply. In the desperation of his mental agony, he repeated the stroke with all his might, and such was the force of the blow that the door flew open as if an engine had been directed against it. Rushing instantly into the house, with a look of wild inquiry, he saw not the object of his search. The apartment in which the bridal festivity had been held was deserted, and his heart throbbed heavily as a most horrible presentiment passed darkly across his mind.

He passed into a second chamber; the mistress was not there. Her maidens were in tears. He inquired, with an expression of agonizing apprehension, where was his beloved. They pointed distractedly towards an enclosure at the back of the house, maintaining an ominous silence. He flew to the spot and found all his worst fears most awfully verified.

Immediately upon her husband's departure for the field, the unhappy bride had ordered the pile to be raised, with the determination of sacrificing herself upon it, according to the custom of her race, should the object of her tenderest attachment perish in the encounter. She knew the disparity of numbers between the hostile parties, and was therefore prepared for the worst. When the distracted bridegroom entered the enclosure in which his devoted sita had erected the funeral pile, with a convulsed countenance and bursting heart he beheld her already upon the burning fabric. The flames were rapidly ascending to do the work of death, while she stood erect and undaunted with an expression of stern determination on her countenance that absolutely appalled him. Her eye gleamed with a portentous energy, and as he entered was riveted upon him with a look of withering scorn. Her clothes were already on fire, and her limbs dreadfully scorched, yet she stirred not a muscle; her whole frame seemed fixed like a rock amid the desert upon which the lightnings flash with harmless impetuosity. The Rahtore approached her hurriedly, but she raised her arm, forbidding his advance. He was in a moment riveted to the spot. He dared not interrupt the voluntary sacrifice to which she was now submitting. Her eye moved not from him, and never for a moment relaxed its expression of indignant disdain.

By this time the fire had made dreadful inroads upon her lovely frame; still she discovered not the slightest indication of an agony too intense and terrible for description. Her features maintained the same fearful immobility. In a few moments her legs gave way and she fell upon her knees, the flames entirely encircling her. Every now and then, however, a gust of wind blew the fire from its victim, and discovered her for an instant with the same expression of lofty indignation marked in every lineament of her majestic countenance. The skin of her arms burst and curled up like a scroll of parchment;* the sinews snapped, but she looked upon the havoc which the flames were making upon her beautiful body with a smile of bitter derision, as if she defied their power to inflict suffering. At length her eyes appeared to start from their sockets; she fell backward into the flames, and a period was put at once to her heroism and her agony.

The miserable Rahtore watched beside the pile until her body was completely consumed, when he gathered the ashes together, and placing them in a jar, deposited it on the hearth of the apartment which had been the scene of the marriage revels. Then putting on the saffron robe,† he sallied forth to meet death and to accomplish his revenge. Not a tear moistened his eyes—they were dry and bloodshot. His heart was marble, and every muscle of his compact frame seemed stiffened into unison with the unbending purpose of his soul. The night was dark as the tone and aspect of his mind. The cry of the prowling jackall was a melody to his ears more musical than the sweet serenade of the bulbul,‡ which he had listened to in the days of his joy. He crept stealthily through the jungle, like a tiger lurking for

---

* I once witnessed a similar circumstance at a Suttee which took place in the neighbourhood of Poonah.

† When a Rajpoot puts on the saffron robe, he devotes himself to death.

‡ The Indian nightingale.

its prey, lest he should be observed by any of the enemy's scouts. He at length gained the tent of his mortal adversary, who had been long hushed in slumber after the fatigues of that sanguinary day.

The Rahtore, covered by the darkness, reached the opening of the tent, which was negligently guarded, as it was known that the adverse party had been cut off to a man, and their chief was even supposed to be among the slain. He found no impediment—all was still as death. He entered. A dim lamp, which threw a heavy ochreous light around, was burning on the ground, near which lay the Hara chief upon a coarse rug, and covered with a common palampore.* A sardonic smile passed over the convulsed features of the Rahtore as he gazed upon the prostrate form before him. Withdrawing his eyes for a moment from his victim, an expiration of the deepest bitterness slowly escaped from his labouring bosom. He drew his sword; it gleamed faintly in the lamp-light. He tore the covering from his sleeping foe, standing over him like an avenging demon to whom the cry of pity would have been at once a mockery and a provocation. The old man started from his sleep, instantly grasped his sabre, but, ere he could raise his arm, he fell a headless trunk at the feet of the vindictive Rahtore.

The noise occasioned by this work of destruction was heard by the guards, who immediately rushed in. When they saw a Rajpoot standing in the safron robe, they but too well knew what had been his purpose, and a single glance sufficed to show how terribly he had accomplished it. He deliberately bestrode the body

---

* Counterpane.

of his prostrate enemy, and, darting a look of fierce defiance at the intruders, pointed with a grim smile at the reeking corpse over which he was standing in ferocious triumph. The guards rushed forward to avenge the death of their chief, and the Rahtore, in the paroxysm of desperation, soon laid three of them dead at his feet. His weapon was raised to immolate another victim, when he received a javelin in the temple and fell dead.

Thus ended this sanguinary feud, of which many instances are recorded equally terrible in the annals of Rajpoot warfare.*

* They who are acquainted with the history of this extraordinary race will not be surprised at the details of this sad narrative.

CHAPTER XV.

GARDEN HOUSES AT LUCKNOW.—PARIAHS.

The day before we quitted Lucknow we paid a visit to the Newaub to take leave and thank him for his hospitality. We were received in a splendid apartment of the palace, in which the prince was seated upon a Persian carpet covered with rich devices, and smoking a hooka through a mouthpiece studded with jewels. He treated us with great complacency and kindness, and, after a few minutes' conversation on indifferent topics, we withdrew. Upon quitting the Newaub, we repaired to the garden of the palace which was laid out with great magnificence and taste.

The buildings represented in the engraving are merely garden-houses, constructed of brick and beautifully stuccoed with chunam; they are raised on chaupoutres,* with steps to ascend from the garden to the first story. They are spacious, having broad terraced roofs, and at each angle a small cupola covered with the same delicate stucco. Some of them are surmounted by an elegant square canopy with curtains depending from the four sides. These canopies are

* Platforms.

supported upon small pointed arches; and here is a delightful retreat from the heat of the noonday sun. The interior of the garden-houses is divided into apartments, which are occupied by the different functionaries to whom the charge of the gardens is committed. Although the exterior effect of these buildings is sufficiently imposing, they nevertheless do not present much attraction to the traveller, except as forming part of the palace of this distinguished city. Though less costly in their structure, it must be allowed that they are more picturesque than some of the grander edifices. In the distance is the mosque before-mentioned, built by Asoph ud Dowlah.

Quitting Lucknow, we proceeded towards Juanpoor. On our route we found some of the large nullahs that intercepted our path so much swollen by the rain which had lately fallen, that we could not cross them without difficulty. At length, by a most simple contrivance we passed over them very securely. From a neighbouring village we obtained a charpoy, or small narrow bed, the legs of which were inserted into four large earthen vessels of a globular shape, with small mouths, called cudjree pots; each aperture was covered by the frame, so as to exclude the access of the water. When launched upon the stream, the charpoy floated buoyantly upon the surface, and we thus easily accomplished our transit, being drawn over upon this slight machine by a rope, together with our palankeens and baggage. This portable bridge we took with us: it was consigned to the care of two coolies,* who were a brace of pariahs, and I could not help noticing, on

* Porters.

one occasion, with a feeling of painful compassion towards these poor outcasts, the indignation with which a high-cast Hindoo dashed an earthen jar of milk upon the ground, and broke it to atoms, merely because the shadow of the pariah had fallen upon it as he passed.

This numerous tribe are in a condition of the most abject degradation; the worst state of bondage would be comparative blessedness if substituted for the position in which they stand among the communities that surround them. They are considered by the higher order of Hindoos, and in fact by every caste above their own, not only utterly despicable in this world, but aliens from the beatitudes of another. The indignities heaped upon them in consequence are repugnant to humanity: nothing can exceed the heartless scorn with which they are everywhere met. They are denied the common social privileges of man, and degraded below the vilest of the brute creation. The pariah is forbidden communion with all but his own immediate tribe, and whatever even his shadow overcasts, belonging to a person of superior rank, is deemed polluted. If it be food of any kind, it is thrown away; if anything of a frangible nature, it is destroyed; and if a thing of value, it is only to be recovered from its contamination by the most rigorous purifications.

These unhappy beings are held in such utter abhorrence by the whole Hindoo population, that the laws of the latter award no punishment for the murder of a pariah, save that of a small fine, and which is seldom enforced, except in very aggravated cases. The occupation of this despised race consists in the

most disgusting offices: they are the scavengers of the cities and villages; they perform all kinds of servile and filthy duties, and from their wretched manner of living are subject to loathsome diseases. So impure are they in the eyes of a Brahmin, that they dare not appear in his presence without subjecting themselves to the penalty of death or some punishment but little short of it. Should a person of any other caste condescend to speak to a pariah, the latter is obliged to place his hand before his mouth, lest the breath of a being so depraved should taint the atmosphere which the former breathes, and thus render him impure. These miserable outcasts are neither allowed to enter a temple nor admitted to the privileges of any religious communion. While the higher order of Hindoo thinks it meritorious to save the life of a noxious reptile, he would esteem it meritorious to destroy a pariah.

Although the Brahmin, who, when spiritualized by mortification and penances, frequently holds himself to be only second to an avatar of his god, looks upon the pariah as a creature unworthy even of those sympathies which he deems to be due to the brute, still, so great is the reverence in which these abjected aliens hold the Brahmins, that they will worship the very ground which they consider to have been hallowed by their footsteps. Scorned as they are by every other class and excluded from all reputable communion with their fellow-men, they are reduced to the necessity of wandering about as vagabonds whom it is held an abomination to relieve and meritorious to spurn. Should the bitterest privations overtake them, they are left unpitied to linger out the agonies of a hopeless existence, or to resort to those desperate modes of obtaining their daily bread which render them still more odious among the communities by whom they are denied the natural privileges of social beings. Thus abandoned, and smarting under the stigma of unmerited degradation, they frequently repair to the jungles, where they conceal themselves from the sight of those who behold them with such indignity, and live in a state of moral desuetude, prowling savagely for human prey, like the beasts of the forest.

Their hand is against every man, and every man's hand is against them. They often have recourse to dacoity, that system of lawless plunder which is carried to excess in India; and when this is the case, they naturally become desperate and ferocious robbers. Is this to be wondered at? Can we be surprised if in their social position they should hold it a law of equity to wage a war of general extermination? Is there not much to be said in extenuation of poor wretches driven, as they are, to the hopelessness of desperation? They sometimes, it is true, wreak a terrible retaliation upon their oppressors, and think themselves justified in doing so. Will it be matter of wonder that the crushed adder should turn and sting? But although they occasionally commit acts of great predal enormity, they nevertheless more commonly submit to dreadful privations with the greatest fortitude, frequently skulking from the jungles, where they have lived upon the fruits of the forest until these have ceased to supply the cravings of nature, and seeking the banks of the Ganges, when, under the cover of night, and with no eye but that of the casual passenger to behold them, they have been known to drag on shore human carcasses that were floating down the stream, and, like the hungry vulture, satisfy the longings of a morbid appetite upon this unnatural provision, while in a state of the most disgusting decomposition.

It is indeed shocking to think that such horrors are to be witnessed in a highly civilized country, the people of which are often eminent for their mildness and humanity. But revolting as is the very contemplation of such a humiliating fact, it will nevertheless appear that this description of cannibalism is not confined to the poor despised pariah.

"I will go a step further," says Mr. Moore, " and say that not only do Hindoos, even Brahmins, eat flesh, but that at least one sect eat human flesh. I know only of one sect, and that I believe few in number, who do this, but there may, for aught I can say, be others, and more numerous. They do not, I conclude, (in our territory assuredly not,) kill human subjects to eat, but they do eat such as they find in or near the Ganges, and perhaps other rivers. The name of the sect I allude to is, I think, Paramahansa, as I have commonly heard it named; and I have received authentic information of individuals of this sect being not very unusually seen about Benares, floating down the river upon a human body, and feeding on it. Nor is this a low despicable tribe, but, on the contrary, esteemed, by themselves at any rate, a very high one. Whether this exaltation be legitimate or assumed by individuals, in consequence of penance or holy and sanctified acts, I am not prepared to state but I believe the latter, as I have known other instances where individuals of different sects, by persevering in extraordinary piety or penance, have been deemed in a state incapable of sin. The holiness of the actor sanctified the act, be it what it may; or, as we say, ' to the pure all things are pure.' But I never heard of these voluptuous saints carrying their devotion or impudence to the disgusting extravagance under our consideration. They are still much respected; more, however, under all their shapes by women than by men.

"I will finish my notice of the Paramahansa by observing that my information stated, that the human brain is judged by these epicurean cannibals as the most delicious morsel of their unsocial banquet." *

In the ninth volume of the Asiatic Researches, in an account by Major Mackenzie of the Jains,—a sect remarkable for their humanity, and it is against the express law of their religion to put any animal to death—there is the following remarkable passage, referring to the Buddhists, who also consider it a deadly sin to take away animal life. It would lead to the inference that these latter are likewise cannibals. "The Jains generally account modestly for all their tenets, and conduct themselves with propriety; and never assert that their bodies are eternal and that there is no God. Nor do they, like the Buddhists, say after death there is no pain in the flesh nor feeling; since it feels not pain nor death, what

* Miscellaneous notice of the Brahmins and Hindoos. Vide Hindoo Pantheon, page 352.

harm is there in feeding upon it when it is necessary to procure health and strength?" If this passage does not go so far as to prove that the Buddhists are cannibals, it is at least a justification of cannibalism.

Dr. Leyden, in his dissertation on the language and literature of the Indo-Chinese nations,* gives an extraordinary account of anthropophagy practised in the island of Sumatra, where the people in general are by no means uncivilized.

"When a man becomes infirm and weary of the world, he is said to invite his own children to eat him. In the season when salt and limes are cheapest, he ascends a tree round which his offspring and friends assemble; and, shaking the tree, they join in a dirge, the burthen of which is this:—the season is come, the fruit is ripe, and it must descend! The victim descends, when those who are nearest and dearest to him, deprive him of life, and devour his remains in a solemn banquet."

The landscape between Lucknow and Juanpoor, especially near the former city, presents at times the same artificial appearance as an English park. Upon our approach to the latter town, several fine old mosques for which it is remarkable, rose sublimely in the distance, affording an agreeable relief to the unvarying aspect of the surrounding scenery. As we approached the bridge they opened in full view before us, and forced from us an exclamation of involuntary admiration. The Atoulah kau Musjid is one of the most highly finished structures of its kind in Hindostan. It is only second in magnificence and in the

* Vide ninth volume of the Asiatic Researches.

costliness of its materials to the celebrated Taje Mahal. And when we remember that it was built full two hundred years before, the expenditure may be considered as falling little short of that laid out upon the more gorgeous structure.

The Atoulah kau Musjid is said to have cost seventy lacs of rupees, or upwards of eight hundred thousand pounds; and the view of this grand edifice fully justifies the supposition that the amount of the outlay has not been exaggerated. This temple is highly venerated by all pious Moslems, who hold it only second in reverence to the Prophet's shrine at Mecca. We were admitted into the interior without the slightest difficulty; for, unlike the Turks, the Mahomedans in India are generally extremely courteous to strangers, and express no repulsive hostility to Christians. The most gorgeous portion of the interior is the central aisle, that rises to a great height, being divided into several stories, and covered by a vast dome which has a panelled ceiling ornamented with very elaborate decorations.* The basement of this aisle represents a square rising to the height of about twenty feet, when the angles are intersected, their number being thereby increased to eight. Here is the termination of the first story, round which there is a gallery divided into recesses, and adorned with the most exquisite tracery. At the termination of the second story, where there is also a gallery similarly decorated, the angles are again intersected and increased to sixteen; each story thus graduating towards circularity until the angles fade before the

* See frontispiece.

eye in the altitude, leaving a perfect circle, the whole terminating in a dome of great extent, and magnificently ornamented. The doorways at the base, of which there are nine, and the cornices above them, are covered with a profusion of minute but admirable architectural embellishments; the floor is beautifully paved with a fine smooth stone almost as closely grained as marble, and much more durable. It has resisted the wear of four centuries without exhibiting the least roughness of surface.

The entrance to this fine mosque is very striking. The external doorway is flanked by two square masses of stone-work which rise, on either side, to the height of at least eighty feet. These buttresses are united by a wall traversing the top of the arch, and surmounted by a parapet enclosing a spacious terrace. The arch of the entrance is sunk several feet beneath the external surface of the stone buttresses, which are embellished at intervals with a rich tracery, in bold relief. The centre of the arch extends as high as the base of the transverse wall, and the spandrels are covered with different devices, skilfully wrought in the solid marble with which they are cased. The stone of which this sacred edifice is built is of so firm a texture and of so durable a quality, that the angles of the various carvings are just as sharp as the first moment they were finished. This mosque has no minarets, and therefore differs, though in no other respect, from the generality of Mahomedan temples. The terrace over the entrance is the spot whence the priest announces the hour of prayer.

CHAPTER XVI.

WHITE ANTS.—BENARES.—INFANTICIDE.

During our stay at Juanpoor, we were so annoyed by white ants, that we were glad to escape from this intolerable nuisance and proceed on our way to Benares. These extraordinary insects are one of the greatest marvels in natural history. They are the most destructive creatures of their size in the universe. Nothing but stone or metal can resist their powers of devastation. They will pass through a whole shelf of books in an incredibly short space of time. In a single night they will make their way into a strong wooden trunk, and ruin everything it contains. I have known them perforate a thick stake of at least ten inches in diameter, leaving nothing but the bark entire, so that what appeared strong enough to support a large building, crumbled at the touch like a piece of tinder. They abound more or less in every part of India, though they prefer a soil where clay is readily to be obtained, as they use vast quantities in the construction of their populous habitations. One of their cantonments will cover a surface of at least fifty square yards, and rises sometimes to the height of twenty feet. In particular districts these are so numerous, that they appear like small villages in ruins dotting the surface of the plain. These singular insects form a community under the government of a king and queen. The population is divided into three classes. The first class comprises the belligerent portion, which are always prepared to defend their habitations from the assaults of an enemy, and they inflict so sharp a wound when intruded upon, as immediately to make the blood copiously flow. The second division includes those which perform all the labours of their community; these build their tenements and repair whatever breaches may be made either by foes or accident. The third class consists of those that propagate. From these they select kings and queens which almost immediately emigrate and erect new states, that shortly become crowded with a busy and destructive population.

When they fix upon an object of destruction they first cover it with a thin coat of clay moistened by their own secretions; under this crust are innumerable passages in which they work unseen, and with the most destructive celerity. Here they labour in perfect security until they consume the whole material, finally leaving nothing but the artificial incrustation with which they had overspread it, and which assumes the exact form of the object destroyed.

" They generally enter the body of a large tree," says an observing traveller, " which has fallen through age or has been thrown down by violence, on the side next the ground, and eat away at their leisure within the bark, without giving themselves the trouble either to cover it on the outside or to replace the wood which they have removed from within, being somehow sensible that there is no necessity for it. These excavated trees have deceived me several times in running; for attempting to step two or three feet high, I might as well have attempted to step upon a cloud, and have come down with such unexpected violence, that besides shaking my teeth and bones almost to dislocation, I have been precipitated head foremost among the neighbouring trees and bushes."*

Their communities are so numerous that the destruction of myriads makes no sensible diminution, and in some ungenial localities, they are such a continual nuisance, as to have a considerable influence upon a man's social comforts. The queen is incredibly prolific and will produce upwards of eighty thousand eggs within twenty-four hours. And what is extraordinary in the civil organization, if I may so say, of this little commonwealth is, that the king and queen have a host of retainers constantly in waiting: as soon as the latter lays her eggs, they are carried to different cells, at a distance from the state apartment, where they are carefully deposited, and when hatched, the new-born insects are attended with the most vigilant circumspection, until able to provide for themselves and share in the labours of their community.

These creatures are so fond of paper that they never fail to make great havoc among the books that happen to be within their reach. The only protection from their depredations is a binding of Russia

---

* See Mr. Smeathman's account of the White Ant, in the seventy-first volume of the Philosophical Transactions.

leather, which they will not touch, being repelled by the strong odour that escapes from this valuable material.

After we quitted Juanpoor nothing occurred worth recording until we came in sight of Benares—that celebrated city called the splendid, containing the most renowned seminaries of Hindoo learning to be found in Hindostan, a more detailed account of which will be found in the first volume of this work. As we approached the city we were induced to moor our budgerow and land, in order that we might witness the Churrack Pooja—one of those revolting inflictions which some particular orders of devotees undergo, together with such unhappy Hindoos as have had the misfortune to lose their caste; the former to enhance their claims to a blessed immortality, the latter to recover that temporal superiority over a large portion of their fellow beings which the well known distinction of caste confers. A man frequently loses his caste by circumstances over which he can have no control, such as the casual contact of a pariah whom he might not have known to be within his vicinity, or eating out of a polluted vessel, though not at the time aware of its pollution.

I once happened to be present when a sepoy, of high caste, falling down in a fit, the military surgeon ordered one of the pariah attendants of the regimental hospital to throw some water over him, in consequence of which none of his class would associate with him, and he was considered to have forfeited the privileges of clanship. The result was, that as soon as the afternoon's parade was over, he put the muzzle of his musket to his head and blew out his brains. Although, however, the distinction upon which the Hindoo so highly prides himself is often thus easily forfeited, it is not to be regained but by undergoing either severe mortification or some terrible infliction, which happened to be the case in the instance I am about to record.

On landing we found a large concourse of people assembled, and forming a circle of about twenty yards in diameter, in the centre of which was a strong pole fixed upright in the ground. On the top of this pole a transverse bamboo, sufficiently strong to sustain the weight of a man, was attached to a moveable pivot, so that it could be swung either vertically or circularly as occasion might require. The insertion of the transverse bamboo was about one-third part from the end, leaving two-thirds on the other side, to which was attached a cord that reached the ground. At the extremity of the shorter division was a pully from which a strong cord depended about the size of a man's middle finger, having two ends, to which were affixed a pair of bright steel hooks. Both the vertical and cross poles were of bamboo, which is extremely tough and difficult to break. When the apparatus was prepared, a Brahmin, who is usually the functionary on these occasions, advanced to the centre of the area, and having anointed the points of the hooks with a small portion of ghee, from a sacred vessel especially set apart for this holy purpose, he beckoned to the person about to undergo this trying ordeal. The penitentiary was a handsome man, in the full vigour of manhood, and had lost his caste by eating interdicted food during a voyage from Calcutta to China, whither he had gone as servant to the captain of the ship.

On perceiving the Brahmin's signal, he advanced without the slightest indication of alarm, but rather with an expression of joy on his countenance, at the idea of being restored to that position among the members of his own peculiar caste, which he had unhappily forfeited. He was stripped to the loins, having nothing on but the cummerbund and a pair of white linen trowsers which reached about halfway down his thigh. He was a muscular man and rather tall:—he came forward with a firm step. Upon reaching the place of expiation, he knelt down under the cord to which the two bright hooks were attached. Gently raising his hands, and clasping them together in a posture of devotion, he continued for a few moments silent, then suddenly elevating his head, declared himself ready to undergo the penance that should release him from the stains of his recent pollution. The moment his assent was announced, a burst of acclamation was heard from the surrounding multitude. The officiating Brahmin then took the hooks, and with a dexterity that showed he was no novice in his sacred vocation, slipped them under the dorsal muscles just beneath the shoulders. This operation was so instantaneously and so adroitly managed, that scarcely a drop of blood followed. Not a muscle of the man's countenance stirred: all his features seemed stiffened into an expression of resolved endurance which imparted a sort of sublime sternness to every lineament. Not even the slightest quiver of his lip was perceptible, and his eye glistened with thrilling lustre as he raised his head after the hooks had been fixed. His resolution was as painful as it was astonishing. At a certain signal from the presiding functionary, he started from his recumbent posture and stood with his head erect, calmly awaiting the consummation of his dreadful penalty. After a short interval he was suddenly raised into the air and swung round with the most frightful velocity by a number of half frantic Hindoos who had stationed themselves for this purpose at the other extremity of the transverse pole. They ran round the area at their utmost speed, yelling and screaming, while their cries were rendered still more discordant by a deafening accompaniment of tomtoms, tobries, kurtauls, and other instruments so familiar to Indian devotees, and which are indispensable on these and similar solemn occasions, producing anything rather than " a concord of sweet sounds."

The velocity with which the poor man was swung round prevented any one from accurately observing his countenance, though, during one or two pauses made by his tormentors, who became shortly fatigued with the violence of their exertions, there was no visible expression of suffering. Had he uttered a cry, it would at once have neutralized the effect of the penance, though I do not think it could have been heard through the din by which this terrible ceremonial was accompanied. The ministering brahmins, however, are said to have a perception of sound so acute on these occasions, that the slightest cry of the victim never escapes their ear.

After this barbarous ceremony had continued for about twenty minutes, the man was let down, the hooks extracted from his back, and he really seemed little or nothing the worse for the torture he must have undergone. He walked steadily forward amid the acclamations of the surrounding multitude, and followed by his friends, who earnestly offered him their congratulations on the recovery of his caste.

Accidents of a very serious nature have been occasionally known to happen during the infliction of these fearful penances, though such occurrences are, I believe, rare. Should the cord chance to break, the suspended person is propelled forward under the influence of such a powerful impulse, that he is invariably killed on the spot. When this occurs, it is imputed to the magnitude of his sins, and he is immediately cast upon the funeral-pile, neither pitied nor lamented. I have heard a circumstance related by a person once present at the ceremony of the Churrack Pooja when the muscles of the back gave way, the penitent being of considerable bulk, and on his being immediately lowered, the mischief was so extensive, that the wretched man died soon after he was released from the hooks. These things are really too dreadful to be permitted in a civilised country; but in India custom is a positive and indeed a paramount law, and is therefore implicitly followed. " Immemorial custom," says their imaginary lawgiver, " is transcendant law, approved in the sacred scripture and in the codes of divine legislators; let every man, therefore, of the three principal classes who has a due reverence for the supreme Spirit which dwells in him, diligently and constantly observe immemorial custom." *

On landing at Benares we passed a ruined bridge over the Bernar, one of the rivers from which the city takes its present name, and pitched our tents near the Bernar pagoda, situated upon the banks of that beautiful stream. From hence the view of Benares, looking up the Ganges, exactly realizes the interesting description given of it by the great Abul Fazil. "Baranassey," says this remarkable man, in the third volume of his history, "commonly called Benares, is a large city situated between two rivers, the Bernar and the Assey; in ancient books it is called Kassey the splendid. It is in the form of a bow, and the river Ganges resembles the bowstring." The truth of this latter part of the description will be at once verified by a reference to the accompanying view of it, taken from the bank of the river near the Bernar pagoda.

This latter structure has not much to recommend it to the notice of travellers, except its picturesque position on the bank of the river. It falls far short of the splendour of many similar sanctuaries of Hindoo devotion; it is, however, an agreeable object, and there is an air of simple antiquity about it which redeems its less attractive features. We had pitched our tents so near it as to be considerably incommoded by the swarms of devotees who frequented it with a most boisterous piety at so early an hour as greatly to interrupt our repose; and the situation, moreover, being exposed to the full action of the sun,

---

* Institutes of Menu, chap. i. sect. 108.

we were soon glad to change our quarters for a locality more agreeable, at least, if not more convenient: we therefore struck our tents, crossed the river, and pitched them opposite to Aurungzebe's mosque, of which a detailed account has been given in a former portion of this work.

In the neighbourhood of this populous city, one of the greatest victories has been achieved over a most barbarous superstition recorded in the history of mankind. It was here that Mr. Duncan first severed the root of an evil which had spread with the most devastating influence over several extensive and populous districts; it was here that the savage custom of infanticide, once so prevalent among a limited, indeed, but very influential portion of the Hindoo population, was finally extinguished, and our benevolent countryman became the saviour of thousands of infants, who have grown up to bless his name and to show the triumph of a moral administration over the barbarous rites of superstition and the errors of prejudice.

The people among whom this horrible custom originally prevailed, and among whom it even now exists, though practised to a comparatively trifling extent, are Rajpoots, who, from the difficulty of providing proper matches for their female children, immolate them upon the altar of a fierce and revolting pride. A Rajpoot never bestows his daughter unless upon one who is not merely her equal in rank, but is likewise able to maintain for her that social superiority which the parent conceives her born to claim; and the horrors of degradation of any kind are so great among this haughty race as to rend asunder, not only the common ties of humanity, but the links of natural affection. Before Mr. Duncan was appointed resident at Benares, now nearly fifty years ago, infanticide prevailed to a deplorable extent among certain Rajpoot tribes residing in this extensive district; and every effort hitherto made by the British government to check a long-established and widely-spreading evil had entirely failed: the vigilance of the magistracy was baffled, and these murders were constantly taking place in defiance of the ties of paternity and the highest obligations of nature. By indefatigable assiduity, by conciliating the prejudices of a haughty and powerful people, and by adopting the most energetic measures, Mr. Duncan eventually succeeded in greatly diminishing, though not in completely eradicating, this evil in the province over which he presided. The moment the extent of his success became known, his benevolent example was followed by others in different parts of the country, with more opposition, indeed, and not certainly for the moment with equally signal success. Colonel Walker, then political resident at Broach, succeeded in a great measure in suppressing this unnatural practice through a large extent of territory. The difficulties which he encountered in realizing his laudable efforts to exterminate so odious a custom from among an influential and enlightened community, are scarcely to be conceived; nevertheless those efforts were eventually crowned with success. The Jarejahs, a tribe among whom infanticide was practised to a dreadful extent, account for its origin as follows.

They relate that a certain powerful Rajah of their caste, who had a daughter of singular beauty and accomplishments, desired his rajgur, or family Brahmin, to affiance her to a prince of desert and rank equal to her own. The rajgur travelled over many countries without discovering a chief who possessed the requisite qualities; for where he found wealth and power combined, personal accomplishments and virtue were defective; and, in like manner, when the advantages of the mind and body were united, those of fortune and rank were wanting. The rajgur returned, and reported to the prince that his mission had not proved successful. This intelligence gave the Rajah much concern, as the Hindoos reckon it to be the first duty of parents to provide suitable husbands for their daughters, and it is reproachful that they should pass the age of puberty without having been affianced and be under the necessity of living in a state of celibacy. The Prince rejected and strongly reprobated every match for his daughter which he conceived inferior to her high rank and perfections. In this dilemma, he consulted his rajgur, and the Brahmin advised him to avoid the censure and disgrace which would attend the princess's remaining unmarried by having recourse to the desperate expedient of putting her to death. The father was at first deaf to the proposal, and remonstrated against the murder of a woman, which, enormous as it is represented in the Sastra,* would be aggravated when committed on his own offspring. The rajgur at length removed the Rajah's scruples by consenting to load himself with

* One of the sacred books of the Hindoos.

the guilt, and to become in his own person responsible for all the consequences of the sin. The princess was accordingly put to death, and female infanticide was from that time practised among the Jarejahs.*

Whether this be really the origin of female infanticide or not, it is certain that the motive for its practice among the Rajpoots is the same—the difficulty of finding suitable matches for their daughters. But, it may naturally be asked, why not allow them to live unmarried? Because among the Hindoos celibacy is considered a family disgrace, and so universal is this feeling, that there is scarcely to be found an unmarried female of high caste throughout the whole extent of the Indian peninsula. Children are affianced to each other in their infancy, when not more than three or four years old, and girls at that tender age are frequently betrothed to very old men, when the match is considered advantageous; so that an old maid is as rare in Hindostan as common in Europe. Mr. Moor, the ingenious author of the Hindoo Pantheon, tells a story sufficiently amusing, and at the same time strongly corroborative of the fact stated.

" Nana Firnavese, prime minister of the Mahratta empire—the Pitt of India—lost his wife in 1796, when he was rather an old man, and as he was infirm withal, it was not expedient that he should marry, as is usual, a mere infant, and his brahminical brethren sought far and near, and for a long time sought in vain, for an unmarried marriageable Brahminee of a

* See Report from Lieutenant-Colonel Alexander Walker, dated Baroda, 15th March 1808, of the measures pursued by him for the suppression of infanticide in Kathywar or Guzerat.

respectable family. At length one was found remote from the metropolis, at Kolapore, near Goa, and he married her. So little, however, was this success calculated upon, that a reason was expected and given for it. It appeared that this lady in her infancy had been afflicted with some personal debility that had prevented her early betrothment; this had suddenly been removed about the time of Nana's predicament, and he was thus deemed fortunate in finding a damsel under such suitable circumstances."

It may seem extraordinary to Europeans, who have been accustomed to hear of the extreme reluctance which the Hindoos feel to destroy animal life, that there should exist among them such savage customs as an intimate acquaintance with their history and social habits will certainly unfold; for, although their moral and civil code, contained in the Institutes of Menu, exhibits in general a system of rigid morality, corporeal forbearance, and an absence of everything like Draconic severity, except in cases of extreme guilt—nevertheless, there is perhaps no country in the world equally civilized where so many sanguinary practices prevail. This is a problem very difficult to solve, except we admit the general solution, which after all is probably the right one, that every faculty of the mind and natural prejudice of the heart yields to the force of custom, which reconciles us to the greatest moral contrarieties.

Infanticide, however, is not confined to Hindostan: it is practised among the modern Chinese, and a reference to Bryant's Analysis of Ancient Mythology will show how extensively human sacrifice prevailed among the ancient Greeks and Romans at a time when they were looked upon as the most civilized people upon earth. It was a well-known decree of the Spartan lawgiver, Lycurgus, whose code was considered merciful compared with the bloody institutes of Draco, that all children born with any deformity should be destroyed. Even the Jews, in the early period of their history, forced their children to pass through the fire of Moloch, thus presenting a most horrible sacrifice to the brazen god of the Ammonites. When children were offered to this sanguinary deity, his statue was heated red-hot, and the wretched victims were placed within its gigantic arms, where they were almost instantly consumed.

"Such," says Bryant, "was the Kronos of the Greeks and the Moloch of the Phœnicians, and nothing can appear more shocking than the sacrifices of the Tyrians and Carthaginians which they performed to this idol; in all emergencies of state, and times of general calamity, they devoted what was most necessary and valuable to them for an offering to the gods, and particularly to Moloch. But, besides these undetermined times of bloodshed, they had particular and prescribed seasons every year, when children were chosen out of the noble and reputable families, as has been before mentioned. If a person had an infant child it was the more liable to be put to death, as being more acceptable to the deity and more efficacious to the general good. Those who were sacrificed to Kronos were thrown into the arms of a brazen idol which stood in the midst of a large fire and was red with heat; the arms of it were stretched out and the hands turned upward, as it were, to receive them, yet sloping downwards, so that they dropped from thence into a glowing furnace. To other gods they were otherwise slaughtered, and, as it is implied, by the very hands of their parents. What can be more horrid to the imagination than to suppose a father leading the dearest of his sons to such an infernal shrine? or a mother the most engaging and affectionate of her daughters, just rising to maturity, to be slaughtered at the altar of Ashtaroth and Baal? Such was their blind zeal, that this was continually practised, and so much of natural affection still left unextinguished as to render the scene ten times more shocking from the tenderness which they seemed to express. They embraced their children with great fondness, encouraged them in the gentlest terms, that they might not be appalled at the sight of the hellish process, and exhorted them to submit with cheerfulness to this fearful operation; if there was any appearance of a tear rising or a cry unawares escaping, the mother smothered it with kisses, that there might not be any show of backwardness or constraint, but the whole be a freewill offering. These cruel endearments over, they stabbed them to the heart, or otherwise opened the sluices of life, and with the blood, warm as it ran, besmeared the altar and the grim visage of their idol. These were the customs which the Israelites learned from the people of Canaan, and for which they were upbraided by the psalmist: 'They did not destroy the nations concerning whom the Lord commanded them, but were mingled among the heathen and learned their works. Yea, they sacrificed their sons and their daughters unto devils and shed innocent blood, even the blood of their sons and of their daughters, whom they sacrificed unto the idols of Canaan, and the land was polluted with blood.'"

Infanticide is to this day practised among some of the ruder tribes of America, in New South Wales and in the South-sea islands, and wherever this practice prevails, female children are the general victims; yet it must be confessed that among the more savage races who destroy their children it commonly arises from a better principle than that which actuates the more civilized. The former almost invariably resort to this barbarous custom from a feeling of humanity, in order to remove their female offspring from the miseries of a destitute existence; for among all savage or semi-barbarous communities the women are so emphatically the drudges of the men, that their lives are an absolute burden to them. Even in their adolescent years, when free from the slavery to which in their puberty they are hopelessly condemned, they have still only the sad prospect of wretchedness before them; and, so fully alive are mothers to the barrenness of their children's joys, that they have been frequently known to destroy them in order to secure them from the hardships which they themselves undergo. But they never destroy their male offspring, knowing that these inherit the chances of a far more endurable condition. The Hindoo, however, has a much less rational excuse, as he puts his daughter to death merely to evade the penalties of an imaginary degradation.

It is said that among the Rajpoots the child was

always destroyed as soon as it was born either by the mother or the nurse; sometimes by opium, sometimes by stratagem; but it appears that since the practice has fallen into desuetude, through the humane endeavours of Mr. Duncan and of those active functionaries who so shortly after followed his meritorious example, thousands of mothers have rejoiced, with a glowing gratitude, to see their daughters growing up around them in the native loveliness of innocence and youth. I can well imagine the anxious mother now looking on her blooming offspring with all the rapture of an affection enhanced by the remembrance of that horrid law of custom which would once have deprived her of so interesting a pledge of conjugal love, and exclaiming in the words of one of her own native poets—

> " Lost in the silvery beam so soft and fair,
> No eye can trace her as she moves along;
> The winds which fan her, heavenly fragrance bear,
> And trace her footsteps in the virgin throng." *

I believe a case of infanticide is now seldom or never heard of, though within the last half century many thousand victims were yearly sacrificed to an arrogant and inhuman prejudice. It is scarcely possible to conceive the indifference with which mothers are said by those who have described the fact, to have put their new-born babes to death—and mothers too who, on other occasions, when their maternal feelings were aroused, have exhibited the most tender

* Broughton's translations from the Popular Poetry of the Hindoos.

yearnings towards their helpless offspring; but the law of an imperious necessity was then considered so binding among this haughty race, that no parent ever thought of opposing it by exhibiting that symptom of opposition which the least expression of parental sensibility would appear to indicate.

As a proof that even Brahmins are not invariably, as is supposed, averse to the destruction of human life, I may mention that there exists a sect called Karara Brahmins, who are said to be under the influence of a demon, to propitiate whom they administer poison to their guests and friends, by which the protection of their evil patron is secured. A story is current in Guzerat that the wife of one of these Brahmins, having besought a boon from the demon whom she served, which was granted, as a token of her gratitude vowed to offer him the acceptable sacrifice of a human victim, and, as this was not otherwise to be safely procured, resolved to select for the sacrifice one about to be endeared to her by ties of the nearest alliance. She therefore fixed upon the destined husband of her only daughter, to whom, however, she was obliged to reveal the horrible secret. On the day before their marriage, the bridegroom was, according to the custom of this sect, invited to a nuptial banquet at the house of the old Brahmin, his bride's father. He came with the bloom of joy upon his countenance, and the freshness of love in his heart, and while the revelry was going on, the mother mixed poison with that portion of the food which was intended for him. This was set apart with a similar portion, but not poisoned, for the bride, and she was commanded by her mother to direct her affianced husband to the fatal mess. The girl horror-struck at the idea of being made the instrument of destroying one whom she tenderly loved, directed him to another share that had been set apart for the father, who eat of the poisoned dish and perished. Thus the wife became a widow, and was obliged to undergo the penalty of all Brahmins' widows by expiating her crime upon the funeral pile, while the young couple married and were happy.

CHAPTER XVII.

RHOTAS GUR.—A SHEEP-EATER.

On quitting Benares, which we did after a halt of a few days, we directed our steps to Rhotas Gur, one of the most romantic spots south of the Himalaya mountains. At a village, about eighteen miles from Benares, where we halted for the day, we were visited by a gaunt, grim-looking Hindoo, of some celebrity in the neighbourhood, which he had acquired, as well as the admiration of his caste, by his capability of devouring a sheep at a single meal. He was a tall, bony person, somewhat past the prime of life, with a thin, wiry frame, and a countenance of the most imperturbable equanimity, though as ugly as a sheep-eater might be expected to be. He was of the Sudra caste, and his companions seemed to entertain a high idea of his singular accomplishment as a most voracious eater. He offered, for a few rupees, to devour an entire sheep, if we would pay for the animal as well as for the different accessories of the meal. There was something so extraordinary in the proposal that we readily acquiesced. We accordingly prepared to witness this marvellous feat of manducation, by purchasing the largest sheep* we could find, which

* Sheep in India are generally very small and lean.

weighed, when prepared for cooking, just thirty-two pounds. We purchased it for one rupee, or about twenty-two pence.

All being now ready, the carnivorous Sudra commenced his extraordinary feast. Having cut off the sheep's head with a single stroke of his sabre and jointed the body in due form, he separated all the meat from the bones, the whole quantity to be devoured amounting to about twenty pounds. This meat he minced very fine, forming it into balls about the size of a small fowl's egg, first mixing with it plenty of spice and curry powder. As soon as the whole was prepared, he fried some of the balls over a fire, which he had previously kindled at the root of a tree, eating and frying till the whole were consumed. At intervals he washed down the meat with copious potations of ghee, which is sometimes so rancid as to be quite disgusting; and this happened to be the case now. After his prodigious meal, the performer was certainly far less active than he had previously been. His meagre body had acquired a considerable degree of rotundity, and although he declared that he felt not the slightest inconvenience, it was evident that he had taken as much as he could hold, and more than was agreeable. He acknowledged that he could not manage to eat a sheep at a meal more than twice in one week, and that this was oftener than he should like to do it.

Extraordinary as such an appetite may appear, it is very much less so than that act of carnivorous barbarity, mentioned by Colonel Mackenzie in the Transactions of the Royal Asiatic Society, where a man is described as devouring a sheep alive, and a series of lithographic illustrations accompanies the description, representing, with a disgusting minuteness of detail, every part of the revolting process.

Although the most rigid Hindoos profess that in their sacred book, they are prohibited from destroying animal life, yet many even of those restrict this prohibition to tame, and especially to what we call domestic animals, assuming the privilege of killing such as are wild. Few of them, however, are so conscientiously punctilious as not to slaughter a sheep or a goat when oppressed by the calls of a sharp appetite, nor do they hesitate on such emergencies to quote some gloss on their sacred scriptures as an authority for the practice under circumstances of necessity. They find it no very difficult matter to make inclination and necessity co-ordinate in their code of moral obligation.

It is indeed certain that in the Institutes of Menu, which contain the whole formula of Hindoo duties, both civil and religious, the killing of animals is, with some limitations, allowed even to Brahmins; and I believe it is only those of the Jain and Buddhist sects who abstain from this practice altogether. The following is an extract to this purport from that celebrated formulary. "Beasts and birds of excellent sort may be slain by Brahmins for sacrifice, or for the sustenance of those whom they are bound to support." Thus it is clear that they are permitted to slay for sustenance as well as for sacrifice. It is a common error that Hindoos may not eat flesh or destroy life; but the prohibition is particular not general. There are, nevertheless, an immense number of prohibited meats from which they abstain with scrupulous particularity.

So rigid are the Jains in observing the mere textual precept which prohibits killing, that they have established lazarettos for the security of vermin of all kinds, and even of noxious reptiles, to whose wants they attend with the most patient attention, and would rather suffer death themselves than press their finger even upon a musquito. It must be confessed that in general the members of this sect are remarkable for their mildness and humanity. Whatever may be the silly qualities of some of their superstitions, they are more than countervailed by traits of the noblest kind, which are by no means discovered to abound among the mass of the Hindo population.

On the third day after quitting Benares we crossed the bridge at Mow, near Bidzee Gur, and ascended the hill. On reaching the fort in which the rebel Cheit Singh had deposited his treasures in 1781, we found it in a state of great dilapidation. This memorable fortification is erected upon a table-land of some extent, considerably elevated above the level of the plain, and inaccessible on all sides but one, where the ascent is extremely tedious. The circumference of the summit, which is protected by a strongly fortified wall, is about two miles; the ground which it encloses is abundantly supplied with water and well cultivated. We were surprised, on observing the strength of the place and the difficulty of approach, that it should have so easily yielded to the assault of the British troops in 1781; but fear and a bad cause seldom find security even behind walls and bulwarks.

On descending the hill, we proceeded to the Eckpouah ghaut,* through an agreeable wood that terminated within a mile of it. As the country opened before us, the prospect was very striking. Immediately below this pass there was a rich dell thickly wooded, and within its dark recesses the tiger and other savage beasts found an undisturbed sanctuary. A deep and rapid nullah foamed beneath, and the dash of its waters faintly caught the ear of the traveller above as they gurgled through the obstructed passages of the wood. On the right were bold precipitous rocks, the scarped summits of which seemed an invulnerable link between the present and remote time; on the left were gently undulating hills, the distance terminating with the valley, through which the river Soane winds its placid course.

At the ghaut we found it difficult for our horses to descend, on account of a lofty rock, which was all but perpendicular and greatly embarrassed our progress. We searched for another path, but could find none: in spite, therefore, of the precipitous nature of the descent, we had no alternative but to attempt it, and fortunately, after much toil, succeeded in reaching the bottom without accident.

In this mountain-pass we caught a black monkey, and as these creatures are rare, we proposed sending it to England the first opportunity that might offer; but unfortunately it escaped, through the negli-

* A ghaut is literally a pass in a mountain, though the word is often used for the mountain itself.

gence of the person to whose care it was intrusted, and who probably favoured its escape in order to get rid of a troublesome charge. Having continually remarked the foot-prints of tigers and other beasts of prey as we advanced, though tolerably well prepared against an irruption from such formidable enemies, we were not without our apprehensions; we, however, saw nothing to molest us, except four large bears, which we surprised in the bed of a dry nullah, and which were glad to escape from so formidable an array as our party presented.

At some short distance from the Eckpouah ghaut there is a huge, misshapen crag, rising full three hundred feet above the level of the plain. Its sides are so nearly perpendicular that there is no possibility of scaling it. This amorphous mass does not at all appear to belong to the spot, but seems as if it had been upheaved from the bosom of the earth by some primeval convulsion of nature. It bears the marks of very remote antiquity, and from its having so unnatural a location, the native geologists ascribe its position there to the period when, according to their cosmogony, the churning of the ocean took place, by which there was such a general dislocation of nature, that rocks were cast upon plains, and vast tracts of land, forming islands, flung into the sea.

In the neighbourhood of Sasseram, where we halted for a day, we found many fine subjects for the pencil, besides the tomb of Shere Shah, engraved in our first volume. The country round exhibits some noble specimens of oriental architecture, both Mahomedan and Hindoo. As we approached Rhotas Gur, the hills presented a great variety of form, with occasionally a sternness and abruptness of aspect exceedingly attractive to the eye, though not very inviting to the footsteps of the traveller. Shere Shah by a stratagem obtained possession of the fort of Rhotas from the last of a long dynasty of Hindoo princes, Rajah Chintamum, whose family had held dominion over this part of the peninsula during a numerous succession of generations. This fort was considered impregnable until it was taken by Shere Shah, who made it a depository for his treasure and the chief residence of his family, until his death, when it probably reverted to its former possessor, as in the year 1575 it was captured from a Hindoo prince, after a severe struggle, by the Mogul emperor, Akbar.

On taking possession of the fort, in a large temple in the upper part of it, Shere Shah found a number of rude idols cut in marble, which he ordered to be flung over the neighbouring precipice, whence they have never been recovered; and for that act of sacrilegious tyranny his name is to this day execrated by all pious Hindoos in the neighbourhood.

The zemeendar of Akbarpoor, a village at the foot of the hill on which the fort of Rhotas stands, very obligingly sent us two or three men to guide us to the summit. We had not proceeded far on our way, which was tedious from the asperity and narrowness of the path, when our progress was interrupted by the gateway of a fortified pass, of which there are several between the base of the hill and the fort. These gateways are immensely strong, and from the steepness of the ascent oppose a formidable barrier to an approaching enemy. It would, indeed, be a matter of no ordinary difficulty to bring artillery to play upon them, and they form a defence impregnable to any common mode of assault; they have, however, yielded to the skill and perseverance of a superior foe.

On reaching the first gateway, the chief guide stopped before the portal, and with a significant air of ceremony silently unwound his turban; then, putting one end of it into the hand of a companion, and placing himself at the other extremity, which he held, the two men stood on either side of the doorway, across which they drew the turban about three feet from the ground. Our obsequious guides then told us that it was customary for travellers to pay toll before entering the portal, as a propitiatory offering to Pollear, the protecting deity of pilgrims and travellers, who without such an oblation might bring us into mischief. Their logic was conclusive; therefore, upon the strength of an appeal so irresistible, we deposited the customary tribute in the outstretched palm of the petitioner, and passed under the gateway into the gorge of the mountain. We entered several similar portals before we reached the summit, which gave us an exalted idea of the former possessors of this strong-hold, who had displayed great sagacity and skill in fortifying a place so well adapted by nature for the purpose of affording an almost perfect security against invasion. At length we entered the fort, which is gained by a flight of winding steps through a gateway, flanked on either hand by a wall of vast thickness that abuts each side upon a precipice. This wall is built of large masses of a most durable stone so strongly cemented together, that there is not the slightest appearance of decay. The masonry is entirely without ornament, but is still very imposing from its stern simplicity and massive strength: it is a fine specimen of ancient military architecture.

The summit of the hill, on which the fort of Rhotas now stands, is about nine hundred feet above the level of the plain. It is the greatest elevation in this part of the country, and commands a grand and extensive prospect. We found the place altogether so agreeable, that we ordered our camp-equipage to be brought to the fort, within which we pitched our tents, and took possession of an old palace then in a state of great dilapidation, yet sufficiently entire to afford us a satisfactory abode for several days. In consequence of its great elevation, we escaped the general annoyance from reptiles to which all persons who inhabit old buildings in India are especially liable; in short, there was nothing to disturb the serenity of our repose save the chattering of legions of monkeys which had colonised the neighbouring glen, inhabiting the trees that grew from the sloping sides of the precipice beneath the fort. These animals, where they congregate in large numbers, are an intolerable annoyance, and their cunning is so profound, that it is difficult to banish them from a spot of which they have once taken possession.

CHAPTER XVIII.

THE FORT OF RHOTAS.—A HINDOO FUNERAL.

The fort of Rhotas, like Bidzee Gur, stands upon the summit of a table hill, but is much more extensive, embracing a circumference of many miles, within which are several villages, and a moderately numerous population. It is everywhere protected by a lofty wall of immense thickness, except where the precipice presents a natural barrier to an invading army. Wherever the mountain upon which the fort stands, originally appeared in the slightest degree accessible, the wall towers above it with an union of massiveness and strength that seems to bid defiance to every human assault. It however yielded, as I have already stated, to the irresistible valour of the Afghan Shere Shah, who conquered the son of the renowned Baber, and father* of the still more renowned Akbar. Shere Shah had the enviable merit of taking, with inconsiderable loss, one of the strongest fortresses in Hindostan.

Beyond the gateway which leads immediately to the principal fortification, are several plain but handsome structures. There are temples, palaces, granaries, besides villages and single houses. The ba-

* Humayun.

zaars are furnished with everything necessary to supply the domestic wants of the people, of whom many never descended to the plains. The walls and the precipices by which they were surrounded being the boundary of their little world, they lived in a sort of Utopian simplicity, circumscribed within the narrow limits of a few miles, beyond which they did not seem to have the slightest desire to emerge. To such primitive minds the happy valley would have been a paradise, though to Rasselas it was a prison. In truth, happiness is not a fugitive that is to be pursued with breathless impatience through a world of perplexity and care. It is as secure to the indolent cenobite as to the busy wanderer; neither may obtain it, and it may visit the hermitage while it shuns the house of concourse. They generally know it best who seek it least; and certain it is that the little community of this romantic hill, if they were not positively happy, appeared contented, and content is so nearly allied to happiness, that they form rather a distinction than a difference.

The prospect around Rhotas Gur, viewed from the highest point about a mile south of the gateway, is of a truly sublime character; scarcely anything can surpass it, except it be the wild and stupendous scenery of the Himalaya mountains. Here are precipices several hundred feet deep, which it makes the brain whirl to look down, and they are so near the perpendicular, without a shrub to break the uniformity of their sheer rocky sides, that, until within a short distance from their termination, there is scarcely

footing for any animal beyond the size of a lizard. Some of them are clothed with wood nearly to the summit; others are bare almost to their base. Towards the bottom, the sides of the mountain are covered with trees of considerable bulk, and these are so infested with monkeys as entirely to banish silence from her primitive dominion. Their incessant gabbling, for clamour and continuance, can only be compared to a disturbed rookery.

In the old palace which we occupied, we were happily beyond the reach of these serenaders, but they never failed to hail our appearance upon the battlements above with peals of their boisterous merriment. We several times amused ourselves with rolling large stones over the precipice, in order to terrify them into silence; but it had quite the contrary effect: for these ponderous projectiles bounded downward with the most fearful impetuosity, crashing amid the trees, and causing such consternation among the monkeys, that their chattering was changed into loud screams of terror. We saw them bounding from branch to branch in such multitudes, that the whole forest seemed alive. We were notwithstanding wanton enough to continue our perilous pastime for a while at the imminent hazard of some of their lives. They, however, adroitly avoided the impending destruction, and were certainly more alarmed than injured; nevertheless, had they been able to expostulate in words, they would, I imagine, have cried out with the frogs in the fable, " this may be sport to you, but it is death to us."

From the elevation of the hill whence we were

amusing ourselves, the country below to the east and south was visible for many miles, and nothing could exceed the beauty of the prospect. The distant plains lay extended before the eye, bounded by the bright blue horizon, glowing under the vivid beams of an ardent sun, and exhibiting all the varying hues of an abundant cultivation. There were several towns and villages scattered over the extensive scene, and to a superficial observer, everything bespoke a happy and thriving population. But these appearances in India are too often fallacious: for while the country round you seems to promise a plentiful harvest to the husbandman, the ryot, or farmer of the soil, having, from the urgency of immediate want, been obliged to mortgage the produce to the more wealthy Zemeendar, has nothing to look forward to in the promising abundance around him but the pittance to be derived from his own labour in aiding to get in the future harvest; thus gathering, in anguish of heart and prostration of spirit, the scanty and bitter fruits of a poorly rewarded industry. In India, the social condition of the husbandman is one of extreme privation and pitiable endurance. The taxes upon the produce are very heavy, and being moreover levied before there is a return upon the sale of the crop, the farmer is almost invariably reduced to the hard necessity of selling it as it stands to the Zemeendar, who generally contrives to grind him down to a hard bargain, and he has no choice left between acceptance or starvation. Thus he sells the labour of months for little or no profit, all but giving it away, in order to meet the demands of a prince under whose government he lives, and the rapacity of the Zemeendar through whose covetousness he starves. This state of domestic misery among the tillers of the land in the most productive country upon earth, is the reason why so few improvements have been here made in husbandry, and why there is so much valuable land unappropriated. There is no stimulus given to exertion, no encouragement to industry, no motive for improvement. The Zemeendar who takes advantage of the immediate necessities of the husbandman, is at no expense for tillage, for he buys the crops upon those terms which distress ever offers to a ready purchaser; so that there really exists no motive to till beyond what the mere hope of obtaining the absolute necessaries of life supplies. For these reasons agriculture is in a very imperfect state, and likely to continue so until there is some encouragement given to predial industry. The agriculturists in India are precisely in the same state they were centuries ago, nor can there be any substantial improvement until there is a change in the social system—until, in short, the condition of those who raise the crops is ameliorated and brought nearer to that of those who enjoy the fruits of the harvest. So prolific is the soil in this genial climate, that it requires very little labour to render it productive; yet more than half the country is a wilderness. Thorns and briars usurp the supremacy of pulse and grain. The prickly pear scatters its rough tenacious arms over vast tracts of territory, where with little toil a plentiful harvest might be gathered in. There is no doubt that under an improved condition of things, millions of acres, which now lie waste, and over which the "golden ear" has never waved, might be made to teem with fruitfulness, and to bless the toil of a miserable and frequently starving population. Famine would never then spread the blight of her horrible devastation over populous and extensive districts, strewing the earth with gastly corpses, and not leaving sufficient of the living to perform the last offices of humanity to the dead. Thousands of carcasses, in every frightful stage of decay, would not then lie uninhumed, scattering pestilence over the land which famine had first filled with lamentation, and loading every passing breeze with the elements of a most summary destruction. These are not circumstances of unusual occurrence: I was myself twice a witness of such scenes during the period of my residence in the East. They were in truth fearfully sad. I have seen the roads strewed with the dead and the dying. I could make these pages the vehicle of the most appalling descriptions, but I forbear. To persons who have resided long in India, those scenes are too familiar. Alas! that such calamities should arise from defective legislation, for this is the great secondary cause of the evil.

During our stay within the fort of Rhotas Gur, a funeral took place in a village at some short distance from our temporary residence, which we availed ourselves of the opportunity of witnessing; and, as we took care not to mix with the procession, there was no objection expressed on the part of the relatives of the deceased to our being present. The body, as is usual on these occasions, was laid upon a charpoy and covered with a crimson palampore, over which was strewed a profusion of red flowers. The procession was tolerably numerous, consisting of the friends and relatives of the deceased, the latter of whom appeared as chief mourners, filling the air with their discordant lamentations. Nearly the whole village joined the mournful cavalcade, in order to pay their last tribute of respect to the remains of a departed brother. Those persons who immediately followed the bier made a dismal wailing, which was every now and then broken by a sort of shrill chorus in praise of the virtues of the dead. This kind of funeral elegy is always chanted on these solemn occasions, and is considered to form a very essential part of Hindoo obsequies, whether the body be disposed of by cremation or sepulture. The dissonance of their loud and elaborate wailings, mixed with the din of tomtoms, horns, and trumpets, defies description.

When the corpse was brought to the spot destined for its consumption, two parallel trenches were dug a few inches deep and about four feet apart; these were crossed by a trench at either end, the whole space forming a parallelogram about six feet long by four wide, each angle being opposite to one of the four cardinal points. The charpoy was then placed upon the ground and the body uncovered. It was in a very advanced state of decomposition, although death had only taken place late the preceding night. Upon the forehead a mark of caste had been distinctly traced, and the mouth was crammed with betel-nut. The flowers were now taken from the coverlet and strewed over the body, to weaken the fetid exhalations which arose powerfully from it and must have been intolerable to those who were in its immediate vicinity; still they did not seem to be inconvenienced, but calmly proceeded with the solemn ceremonial. Within the square which had been formed, certain mystic rites took place to propitiate the spirits supposed to preside over sepulchres and to have an influence upon the happiness or misery of departed souls. When these were completed, the body was borne towards the pile, which had been carefully erected on a spot previously consecrated for the occasion by the officiating Brahmin. It consisted of large branches of the mango-tree, well besmeared with ghee, rising about two feet and a half from the ground. It was squared with great exactness and regularity, forming a compact body, and the wood was so skilfully disposed that few or no interstices were apparent.

The corpse was now laid upon the pile by four pariahs, who alone touch dead bodies in India; for the contact with a corpse is held by all other castes to be a pollution from which no one can be purified but by undergoing the severest mortifications. It is on such occasions only that the poor pariah is tolerated, and this because his services are indispensable; though even then no rigid Hindoo will approach him so near as to run the risk of coming even within the reach of his shadow. The principal mourner, who I understood was father of the deceased, as soon as the pariahs had retired, approached with a lighted torch in his right hand and a vessel of water on his left shoulder. On reaching the sacred platform on which were deposited the remains of an only son, he turned his back towards it, applied the torch to the combustibles underneath, his eyes the while directed towards heaven, dropped the vessel of water on the ground as soon as he heard the crackling of the flames, then darted off as if he had been pursued by some malignant spirit. The fire kindled with great rapidity; in a few moments the body was enveloped in flames which burned so ardently that it was shortly consumed. The pyre had been previously strewed with unguents and other inflammable substances, in order to accelerate this solemn conclusion of the funeral ceremony. Letting fall the water-vessel is an ancient superstitious test never, I believe, omitted on these melancholy occasions. The idea of this credulous people is, that if it does not break in falling, another of the family will die before the year expires; but that if it breaks—and this seldom fails to happen, from the violence with which they let it fall—the family is secure from such a calamity.

The moment the torch is applied to the pile, the party upon whom it devolves to perform this part of the ceremony rushes from the spot to the nearest tank, into which he instantly plunges, in order as soon as possible to purify himself from the contamination which he is supposed to have imbibed from so near a contact with a corpse. With somewhat less celerity, but following close upon his steps, the rest of the mourners on this occasion repaired to the same tank, where they also underwent the customary purifications. The body being consumed, the ashes were carefully collected and deposited in a large earthen jar, there to remain until an opportunity should offer of casting them upon the sacred waters of the Ganges, which, according to the Hindoo creed, having their source in heaven, will waft them thither,* when those senseless atoms shall be reunited to the disembodied spirit and enjoy with it an immortality of uninterrupted beatitude.

Upon these solemn occasions the ministering Brahmin exacts a considerable fee. From a family in but moderate circumstances he would think a hundred rupees no more than a reasonable demand; and whatever he does demand is paid without a murmur on the supposition that so sacred a person cannot be guilty of extortion. Funerals therefore, where the parties can afford to pay, are always attended with great expense. There was no suttee in this instance, although the deceased left a young widow; that barbarous custom having been almost abolished in this part of the country.

Sonnerat mentions that in some places the widow, instead of burning herself on the husband's funeral-pile, buries herself alive, in order to be immediately united to him in paradise. " When they are buried alive," says this observing traveller, " the same ceremonies are observed before they are conducted to the place of interment as when they burn themselves. So soon as the person who is the object of the sacrifice has arrived, she descends into a place of the form of a small cellar, and takes the body of her husband in her arms. The ditch is immediately filled with earth up to the woman's neck; a carpet is laid before her to

* The Hindoos imagine that as the Ganges has its source in heaven, its waters finally return thither, after purifying the souls of men upon earth.

prevent the horrors of death from being perceived, and that the sight may not frighten other women, they give her something in a shell, which is doubtless poison, and the ceremony concludes by twisting her neck, which they do with surprising dexterity."

On the day which followed the funeral we were out with our guns, when one of the party shot a large vulture that had perched upon the carcase of a dead sheep, and was certainly doing the neighbourhood a benefit by removing the nuisance. As soon as the bird was shot, it fell and turned upon its back; but, struggling a good deal, two of the attendants, of which each person of our party had one, were ordered to despatch it with bamboos. This was accordingly done, and, after receiving several severe blows upon the head, it appeared to be quite dead; one of the men then took it upon his shoulder, and we pursued our sport. We were out several hours, the vulture hanging all the while from the shoulder of the man apparently lifeless, its eyes closed and its head much lacerated by the shot and the strokes from the bamboos. Upon our return, the man who carried the vulture, glad to get rid of his burden, (for these birds will sometimes weigh as much as thirty pounds) flung it upon the ground with a force of itself sufficient to kill it; but to our surprise it seemed to be reanimated by the shock; for after opening its eyes, it suddenly turned, and was on its legs in a moment. Advancing a step or two, it stretched out its wings, rose heavily into the air, continuing to rise until it was entirely lost to our view in the distance. We were all so much astonished at thus so unexpectedly beholding the dead alive, that no one thought of making an attempt to prevent its escape. The tenaciousness of life which the vulture possesses, as this anecdote will show, is almost incredible; and so great is its rapacity, that when engaged in devouring its prey, it will allow a person to approach and seize it, though this is at all times a dangerous experiment.

CHAPTER XIX.

HINDOO TEMPLE AT MUDDENPOOR.

Quitting Rhotas Gur, on our way to Patna, we halted at Gyah, where there are several majestic ruins. At Muddenpoor, a village in the neighbourhood of Gyah, we visited a Hindoo temple, formerly in high repute, though now in a state of dilapidation. There are several small trees growing out of the tower, which rises to a great height above the body of the building, and has four elliptical sides with convex surfaces. It is divided into two stories, and surmounted by a small fluted dome, which makes a graceful termination. The main edifice is square, and adorned with two handsome porticos, one at the eastern, the other at the western extremity. The common entrance is on the south side, through a narrow doorway, over which are some rude carvings. On the foreground, about twenty yards from the south-western angle of the building, is an elegant but massy stone column from fifteen to twenty feet high:—for what purpose it was erected does not now appear to be known. It is hexagonal for the first four feet from the base, when the squares increase in number; but towards the top the pillar is perfectly round, and surmounted by a plain square capital.

This temple, which is built without cement, is supposed to be of extreme antiquity, and its appearance fully justifies the supposition. It stands upon an eminence at some distance from the public road, commanding an extensive and beautiful view of the surrounding country. The hill, though not lofty, is troublesome to ascend; for in consequence of the immense number of persons who still visit this sacred shrine, either from curiosity or devotion, the surface of the rock through which the road is cut is so worn as to render it quite slippery, and to persons unaccustomed to such a ticklish ascent, it is altogether impracticable without assistance from those whom habit has enabled to surmount the difficulty. Nevertheless, when the summit is gained, the traveller's toil is abundantly repaid by the splendid prospect before him, which however is so common in India that it soon ceases to be a novelty, though it cannot cease to give delight. The view from this spot is scarcely inferior to that seen from the summit of Rhotas Gur.

The Brahmins who attend the temple are esteemed very holy persons, and the sanctuary, though in a state of dilapidation, is resorted to by pilgrims from a great distance. It is dedicated to Vishnoo, and is frequently the scene of the most absurd superstitions; yet in spite of the foolish rites to which long established custom has imparted the authority and obligation of law, some of the doctrines taught in these heathen tabernacles are such as would not disgrace a Christian preacher. They inculcate a highly pure morality, and wherever this is infringed, under the sanctions of interested teachers, it is a viola-

tion of the pure Hindoo creed, which, when divested of its corruptions and false glosses, is by no means so free from "spiritual discernment," as is generally supposed. Although, perhaps, there is no country in the world where religion has been exposed to so many gross and monstrous corruptions, there may nevertheless be found beautiful lessons of wisdom and practical virtue even in those Brahminical writings which are accessible to Europeans; while the esoteric precepts of such among their sacred books, as are sealed to all but the privileged few, are said by learned Christians, who have been made acquainted with their mysteries, to contain doctrines so pure and wise, as to be second only to the oracles of inspiration.

He could have been no ordinary teacher who wrote the following. "Let the motive be in the deed and not in the event. Be not one whose motive for action is the hope of reward. Let not thy life be spent in inaction. Depend upon application, perform thy duty, abandon all thought of the consequence, and make the event equal, whether it terminate in good or evil, for such an equality is called yog.* Seek an asylum then in wisdom alone; for the miserable and unhappy are so on account of the event of things. Men who are endued with true wisdom are unmindful of good or evil in this world. Study then to obtain this application of thy understanding, for such application in business is a precious art."† Again, "There is no-

---

* A Sanscreet word, which, says Sir Charles Wilkins, we have none in our language to express. It is nearly synonymous with devotion.

† Bhagvat Geeta, Lecture II.

thing in this world to be compared with wisdom for purity. He who is perfected by practice, in due time findeth it in his own soul. He who hath faith findeth wisdom, and, above all, he who hath gotten the better of his passions; and having obtained this spiritual wisdom, he shortly enjoyeth superior happiness; whilst the ignorant and the man without faith, whose spirit is full of doubt, is lost. Neither this world nor that which is above, nor happiness, can be enjoyed by a man of a doubting mind. The human actions have no power to confine the spiritual mind, which by study hath forsaken works, and which by wisdom hath cut asunder the bonds of doubt." *

We should form altogether a very unjust estimate of the intellectual qualifications of Hindoo teachers, if we tested them by those vulgar superstitions which are constantly presented to the traveller's eye in their numerous temples. These are frequently nothing more than the juggles of an interested priesthood, from which, indeed, the religion of Christian countries is not entirely free. The besotted notions so commonly instilled into the mind of the ignorant Hindoo are as far removed from the spirit of his ritual, as the mummeries sanctioned by the Roman Catholic priesthood are from the purity of those doctrines promulgated by the chosen ministers of the Christian Lawgiver. Wherever religion is taught to be a mystery too subtle for the penetration of common minds, and thus kept from the mental scrutiny of the vulgar; — where it is left to be expounded by a few interested teachers, who derive more temporal profit from prac-

* Bhagvat Geeta, Lecture IV.

tising on the credulity of their hearers, than in opening their eyes to the truth — it will naturally be corrupted; and nothing is too monstrous for ignorant credulity to receive.* Ignorance being naturally attached to the marvellous is consequently inclined to superstition, and thus, in order to satisfy this morbidly spiritual appetite, the attributes of the Deity have been personified, and a host of idols offered to human adoration, under the assumed sanction of a sacred name. The Divinity is so constantly associated with human actions and human infirmities, as to represent an Almighty monster of iniquity, possessing the repugnant qualities of Omnipotence both in good and in evil.

Such views of him are, alas! but too grateful to the feelings of corrupt minds; for we may easily imagine it is no difficult matter for men inherently depraved to persuade themselves that a God, who can be the great exemplar of vicious acts, will not be backward to pardon in others what his own conduct justifies; and therefore this assumed sanction of vice in the Creator cannot fail to render it more palatable to the heart of the creature. The implicit reliance which the ignorant among the Hindoos place upon their priests, who are often as corrupt as they are illiterate, is the chief cause of that barbarous idolatry in which they are still involved, and which has hitherto bid defiance to the most zealous endeavours of our missionaries.

* It is a general belief among the Hindoo vulgar, that no one has a chance of happiness in the next life, if he neglect to give alms to the Brahmins.

Monstrous as the complicated mythology of Hindostan may appear to those who cannot discover the spiritual inference through the mythic adaptation, the Brahminical religion, when divested of its exaggerated fables and allegories, amounts simply to this: that God is eternal, omnipotent, and infinitely wise; the source of all good, and the consummation of all perfection. As he had no beginning, so neither can he have an end, since that to have an end, which has no beginning, would at once involve a contradiction and an impossibility. He is without body, parts, or passions; permeating all space; the antithesis of evil, which he will eventually overcome; an omnipotent, just, and merciful God. He is the creator of all things, the sustainer of all things, and nothing is hid from his scrutiny. Past and future are to him everlastingly present, and his ubiquity enables him to comprehend all things within himself. As he is infinitely merciful, so is he infinitely just, and therefore eternally punishes the wicked as well as everlastingly rewards the good.

The Brahmins further believe that at the time fixed in his eternal decrees, God will destroy this world by fire. They place implicit faith in the influence of inferior divinities, which are subservient to the one Almighty, who wills nevertheless that divine homage, though different from that which is offered to himself, should be paid to them as his accredited vicegerents to whom he has appointed especial functions upon earth. These agents are extremely numerous, and it is in consequence of the homage paid to them that so many corruptions have crept in to destroy the purity of the primitive worship. The doctrine of the metempsychosis is one to which I believe the different Hindoo sects unanimously subscribe. They hold that immediately after death the soul is wafted into the presence of its eternal judge, who passes sentence upon it, condemning it to everlasting happiness or misery according to its spiritual purity or pollution upon earth. If it be condemned to suffer, after an expiation of ages it returns to the world it has quitted and assumes a bestial incarnation. During a succession of lives it takes possession of the bodies of several beasts of progressively higher grades, and thus gradually advances in the scale of animal improvement. When the process of personal atonement has been so far completed, it passes into the frame of a man, still migrating from one human body to another more holy and increasing in spiritual purity until the crimes committed in a former state of existence have been sufficiently expiated, when it is released from its hard bondage of probation, received into the celestial paradise and absorbed into the Deity.

Before we left Gyah we went into the woods with our guns in search of game, a pastime so common in India, that the traveller scarcely passes a day on his journey without enjoying it. On the present occasion a large hog was shot, but did not yield without making a fierce resistance; not until it had received fourteen balls in its body from different guns, did it finally relinquish the hard struggle for life. We left the carcass close by the edge of a jungle, intending on our return to deprive it of its head, and bear this to our tents as a trophy. We continued our sport but shot nothing except a few black partridges and a couple of hares, the latter of which in this country are generally hard and coarse. Upon our return to the spot where we had left the hog, which had not been killed above two hours, we were astonished to find that not an atom of flesh remained on its bones. During our absence the vultures had descended upon the carcase and completely devoured it, though in the most extraordinary manner. When we approached it appeared to be perfectly entire, but upon closer inspection we found the skin to be filled with only bones and air. The hide of the animal was so tough, that the vultures could make no impression upon it; they had therefore insinuated their beaks through the holes made by the balls in the boar's body, gradually enlarging the orifice until they obtained admission for their heads, when with their usual voracity they tore from the bones and skin every morsel of flesh, and shortly swallowed the whole. The entrails were also consumed, so that there remained little more of the dead hog than an inflated skin, which two of our attendants bore away, no doubt gratified at the vultures' ingenuity, since it had greatly diminished their burthen.

The vulture is said to have a keenness of scent so extraordinary as to be sensible of the effluvium of putrid flesh at the distance of more than a mile. Certain it is, that if an animal of any bulk is destroyed and left on the ground, though there should be no vulture in sight at the moment of its destruction, within the space of half an hour it will be covered with these hungry spoilers, which never quit it while a morsel of the carcass remains. When they scent a piece of carrion they immediately congregate in large bodies, make several gyrations in the air over the spot, and then descend upon their prey. They may frequently be seen soaring on the watch at an immense height in the air, and a dead body never escapes either the quickness of their sight or the keenness of their scent. These birds are so voracious, that they have frequently been known to attack distempered cattle and destroy them. If a buffalo happens to have a sore, they will perch upon its back and begin to feed upon it, and, notwithstanding its strength and fierceness, they will continue the assault, one perching on the animal's head and flapping its wings over its eyes, while others fix upon the diseased part, until, worn out with fatigue and suffering, it becomes at length an easy prey to these indefatigable destroyers. The vulture is generally about the size of a large turkey, though some have been known to weigh upwards of thirty pounds. It is very serviceable in hot climates in removing putrid substances, which would else expose the country to the continual visitation of pestilence: in fact, but for these disgusting birds, every region within the tropics would soon be depopulated;—they annually save thousands of human lives.

CHAPTER XX.

BODE GYAH.—BUDDHIST TEMPLE.—BUDDHISM.

From Gyah we proceeded a few miles out of our direct route to Bode Gyah, where there is one of the most celebrated Buddhist temples to be found in Hindostan; it is still an imposing structure, though the ravages of time are visible in several parts of it. The body of the building is a massy square, in the neighbourhood of which are alto-reliefs finely chiselled; they are masterpieces of ancient oriental art. The anatomical proportions are such as show that those masters by whom they were executed had studied the human figure with no common attention. These sculptures have all the reality of life in the attitude and action which they represent, having more grace than the Egyptian, and more action than the Greek, nor are they much inferior to the latter in beauty of proportion and vigour of outline. The tower of this temple rises from the body of the structure, covering the entire square, and gradually diminishing in its elevation until it terminates in a tall columnar top with a round projecting base. On the walls are rich masses of bass-relief, carved with consummate taste and skill. The entrance is through a dilapidated portico, to which you ascend by a broken flight of steps.

On either side is an unseemly mound of earth which has been suffered to accumulate, somewhat diminishing to the eye the beautiful proportions of the building.

The architectural features of this temple are so unlike anything else in the country round it, that an appearance of great antiquity is thus imparted to it, and the conjecture fairly justified that all the other edifices in the neighbourhood are of a much more modern date, although the pagoda at Muddenpoor, near Gyah, has the reputation of being extremely ancient. Colonel Todd, indeed, asserts that in India there are no fine specimens of sculpture, for which the neighbourhood of Bode Gyah is at present pre-eminently distinguished, before the tenth century; but upon what data he grounds his assertion is somewhat problematical. His arguments are to me by no means conclusive, and before he can establish this new theory, he must advance something more tangible than the hypothesis of even a very enterprising traveller, an eloquent writer, an acute reasoner, and an amiable man. He is each and all; I have read his volumes with admiration and respect, and feel deeply his debtor for the information they have afforded me. With regard, however, to his hypothesis, it is to my mind sufficiently negatived by the fact that fine sculpture is now seen on those temples to which the highest authorities ascribe an existence long anterior to the tenth century.

The temple at Bode Gyah is entirely deserted; years have rolled away since the knee of the worshipper has bent before its altars. The priest is no longer there to receive and console the pilgrim; no devotees throng its aisles—no offerings are made at its shrines. It has become a scene of gloomy desolation, a forsaken sanctuary, a shelter for the foxbat and the serpent. At a short distance to the left of the building there is a remarkable stone, upwards of six feet in diameter, representing the chackra of Vishnoo, most exquisitely carved in fine bas-relief; indeed, so great is the knowledge of art displayed in these carvings and the adaptation of that knowledge to the subjects they exhibit, that it would be difficult to find a specimen of modern sculpture of a similar character that could surpass them. The chackra represented by this stone is a missile with which the forefinger of Vishnoo's main righthand, for he has four hands, is armed. It is a sort of discus or quoit, the periphery terminating in a keen edge; and this, when hurled from the finger of the deity, carried death and desolation before it.

There are few inhabitants in the neighbourhood of this magnificent structure, which, in spite of neglect, desertion, and the dilapidations of ages, seems formed, like the pyramids, to endure until it shall be finally toppled down amid

" The wreck of matter and the crush of worlds."

About a mile from Bode Gyah there is an immense pile of building which forms one solid mass of cemented brick, but for what purpose it was erected no one can now surmise. As a contrast to the ancient Hindoo architecture exhibited in this temple, the reader is referred to a grand mosque in the Coimbatoor district, built by Hyder Ally, and perhaps the finest specimen of modern Mahomedan architecture in India.

The one has not been erected above sixty years, the other has perhaps existed nearly half as many centuries. Nothing can be more perfectly opposite than the two styles, and yet both are perfect in their kind.

I shall devote the remainder of this chapter to a brief account of that remarkable sect which raised the splendid temple at Bode Gyah. The Brahminical religion by consecrating the hereditary principles of caste, by declaring there was no passage from one caste to another, by proclaiming that all men who were not of the Aryas, were Mlêchha, or barbarians, fixed limits to its own progress that could not be passed. When once it was established that crimes committed in a previous state of existence irrevocably determined the fate of men in the present life; that he who was born a Mlêchha must remain a Mlêchha, whatever were his virtues, and that he who was born an Arya should continue an Arya whatever were his vices, there could be no motive to conversion; the very attempts to make proselytes must have been regarded as criminal. Two results necessarily followed from such a system. The Aryas seized supremacy as a matter of right; the Mlêchhas were ready to receive with pleasure the first daring innovator that would denounce as unfounded the dogmas which sentenced them to hopeless degradation.

We must not imagine that the system of caste belonged exclusively to India: on the contrary, we have strong proof that it prevailed over the greater part of central and western Asia. In Persia, for instance, the Medes claimed to be Aryas, and under that pretext demanded submission from the Persians.

It is singular that certain history begins for almost every nation of the East, at the moment when the chains of caste were broken; and the sixth century before Christ, in which Cyrus commenced the great religious and political revolutions which Darius Hystaspes and Zoroaster consummated, is an important era not merely for Persia, but for India, for Ceylon, and the Indo-Chinese nations.

We know the fact of the introduction of a new religion into Persia and central Asia about this period; a religion more universal in its character than the Brahminical, which recognized no hereditary disqualifications, which either totally abolished or greatly modified the system of caste, and which, as a necessary consequence, elevated the character of saints and prophets, above that of the priestly tribe. Derived from a creed strictly exclusive, the new religion retained no trace of this characteristic of its parent, and yet preserved almost every other. It spread rapidly over Eastern Asia; but in India, the country of its native birth, it was met by the fierce hostility of those whose supremacy rested on the system of caste, and it fell in the encounter.

The new religion thus established in the countries round India received the name of Buddhism, from the word Buddha, which signifies a "holy person." It borrowed from Brahminism, its mythology, its philosophy, and a part of its rites and ceremonies; but it substituted for an hereditary priesthood, an organized hierarchy and monastic institutions.

In speaking of Buddhism, too much caution cannot be used; perhaps there is no subject on which so

much nonsense has been written by those who lay aside research for conjecture. There have even been found some who assert that it is a more recent religion than Brahminism, though the marks of its derivative character are stamped on every portion both of its faith and practice; though its creed can be deduced from Brahminism by logical sequence. In the fifth section of Mr. Colebrook's Essay on the Philosophy of the Hindoos, it will be seen that in the Upanishads or terminating sections of the Vedas, an ascetic and contemplative life is recommended as the true means of salvation. Such a doctrine produced a race of anchorites possessing more influence over the vulgar than the Brahmins, just as with the Jews the schools of the prophets possessed more authority than the descendants of Aaron. A consequence of the recommendation of contemplative life, recognized indeed in the Vedas themselves, is that a greater authority will be attributed to the interior revelations of the conscience, than to the revelations in the Sacred books, of which the priests are the hereditary guardians; and this principle followed out, is manifestly subversive of caste, because it elevates the anchorite of whatever tribe he may be, above the Brahmin. In fact, some of the present Hindoo schools of philosophy have not hesitated to go the entire length of preferring the revelations within the soul, discovered by profound meditation, to the Vedas or Scriptures.

The praise of asceticism, and especially the belief in the mysterious revelations made to the ascetic, necessarily led to the attribution of divine qualities to the sages who retired from the busy haunts of men, to enjoy divine meditations in the wilderness. There needed only an individual of this class to appear, endowed with superior intelligence and favoured by circumstances, to collect admirers, followers, disciples; to become the founder of a new religion, and perhaps the reformer of the political system. The Brahmins, relying on their prescriptive power, he would probably find at once arrogant and indolent; he would discover the lower classes deprived of knowledge by their superiors, and at the same time he would see this ignorance made an excuse for withholding their civil rights. His first appeal would be made to the poor, and it would be eagerly welcomed by a host of partisans. Such a reformer was found in the person of the Buddha Sakia Muni, that is to say, the holy hermit Sakia. The dates of his appearance vary considerably, not only in the different Buddhist nations, but in the histories of each nation. Schmidt, in his Mongolian History, says that he found among the Tibetans thirteen different dates, of which the extremes are more than a thousand years asunder. The latest of these eras is the one adopted by the Singhalese, which places Sakia between the years B. C. 638 and 542.

In accordance with the merits attributed to a life of celibacy, the Buddhists believe that Sakia was born of a pure virgin, that he was a divine incarnation, and that on his appearance in the world, all the inferior deities paid him homage. His supposed father was king of Mogadha, in Southern India, and was so delighted with the beauty of the boy, that he declared him heir to his kingdom.

When Sakia grew up, he was deeply affected by the sight of human misery, and in spite of every remonstrance, resolved to lay aside the splendours of royalty and lead the life of a hermit. Several of the young nobles imitated his example and professed themselves his disciples. For many years, Sakia lived in the desert, absorbed in meditation, scarcely paying any attention to the common necessaries of life, and evincing his humility by refusing the services and homage of his disciples. From hence he removed to a still more solitary place, where he was assailed by several temptations, over all of which he triumphed. Being now persuaded that he had subdued all human lusts, he prepared to publish a new system of faith; but before commencing the publication he underwent a series of fasts and penances for forty-nine days. His first sermon to his disciples on the origin and necessity of faith, may be regarded as a brief summary of the principal doctrines of Buddhism.

" The universal state of misery, that is, the present world, is the first truth; the path of salvation is the second truth; the temptation to which we are exposed is the third truth; and the mode of overcoming temptation is the fourth truth." He then proceeds to explain the signification of these truths in the following terms. " In the course of human life no moment of pleasure equals that in which we acquire cognizance of the truth; thus I name this world, a true state of misery, and the practice of the precepts of faith the greatest happiness. Consider the fourfold condition of man; the pains attending his birth; the diseases he has to encounter in the course of his life; the miserable condition of his old age, and the calamity of death. As years increase, his skin becomes dry and wrinkled like an old parchment; the flesh upon his bones withers and wastes away; the blood in his veins flows sluggishly; his body bends towards the ground; his sight begins to fail, and even mountains are scarcely apparent to his weak eyes; the sense of hearing is so lost that trumpets sound for him in vain; the mouth loses its teeth; and fragrance is wasted on his decayed sense of smelling. The diminution of his bodily strength compels him to have recourse to a staff for support, the faculties of the soul change into distraction and forgetfulness." He thus at great length enumerates all the possible evils to which man is subject, and concludes by declaring that belief in the Buddha is the sure path of salvation.

The path of salvation can scarcely be explained without entering very deeply into the mysteries of Indian metaphysics. All religions that do not profess to be founded on a special revelation, must of necessity be Pantheistic, because Pantheism is the natural result to which we are led by unassisted reason. But, few have been content to stop here: in most instances men look beyond the material and changeable world, for that which is immaterial and unchangeable. The Buddhists arrive at this notion by abstracting all the attributes that would imply limitation until nothing is left but the simple idea of existence. This remote abstraction, which has been well termed "the something-nothing," they regard as the supreme God. The world and its deceptive appearances have only an illusive existence; they were produced by beings or agencies that emanated in the fourth degree from the Supreme Being or Sunya. Man attributes to these worldly appearances a reality which they do not possess, regards things as good which are truly evil, allows himself to be overcome by the vicissitudes of life, and recognizes not his original destination. He must, then, detach his soul from all the objects which excite passions or desires, he must devote himself to profound contemplation, to arrive at that intuitive science, that state of the soul in which it recognizes the nature of those fallacies, and thus acquires mastery over the world and its illusions. The soul thus divested of worldly passions and affections, becomes itself a Buddha. After death it passes into the state of nirwana, when it is wholly absorbed in the Sunya, and perfectly identified with the Deity.

This is the best account of Sakia's doctrine that can be deduced from the mysticism with which either he or his followers have veiled the system, a mysticism of which the reader may judge from the following specimen.

"Buddha says, my religion or law consists in thinking the unconceivable thought; my religion consists in going the unpassable way; my religion consists in speaking the ineffable word; my religion consists in practising the unpracticable practice."

Sakia spent his whole life in diffusing his doctrines, but as he seems never to have formally embodied his followers into a sect, he escaped persecution. When his eightieth year was passed, he assembled his principal disciples, and recommended them to form themselves into a separate society after his death. He told them that such a measure would undoubtedly expose them to fierce persecution, and recommended them when the hour of distress and danger arrived, to seek a refuge in the mountains north of India. He advised them also to prepare images of his person, the sight of which would serve to fortify their faith. Statues were accordingly executed, representing the Buddha at different periods of his life. The most celebrated of these exhibits him sitting with his right hand on his knee, his left holding a string of beads, and his hair which had not been cut during his residence in the wilderness, clustered in curls over his brow.

Soon after this he obtained nirwana without suffering the pains of death. The Buddhists show the print of his foot on several mountains. He impressed it just before his ascent into heaven; and a representation of this foot-print is usually found in every Buddhist temple.

It is very difficult to separate truth from falsehood in this story of Sakia; we cannot even determine whether it was his design to found a sect, or whether he merely recommended the ascetic philosophy, the doctrines of which carried to the extreme by his followers, necessarily formed a new religion. Like most men who have given a new direction to the religious ideas of his contemporaries, he was less an inventor than a collector of dogmas; developing more plainly and forcibly what many before him had often thought and what some had obscurely expressed. When in a later age his followers came to write the life of one who had preached such vast reforms as the abolition of caste, at least so far as religion was concerned, of hereditary priesthood, and of bloody sacrifices, they were astounded at the vast amount of change proposed, and naturally ascribed it to superhuman intellect; they were thus tempted to interweave in Sakia's life the legends of Rama and Krishna, the more especially as when he quitted Brahminism he brought with him the greater part of its mythology, though he abolished all its practice.

The Buddhists were a powerful sect in India, when Alexander the Great appeared on its north-western frontier; but soon after that event, the Brahmins discovered that the progress of the new sect threatened the ruin of their power. It is not easy to ascertain when persecution began; but Professor Wilson is of opinion that the great effort for the suppression of Buddhism was made in the fifth and sixth centuries of our era. In northern India, the Buddhists seem to have made some stand, for the Brahmins never possessed so much influence there as in other parts of the Peninsula, and hence in that quarter, the remains of Buddhist temples are by no means infrequent.

Assailed by the Mahomedans on one side, and the Brahmins on the other, few, if any Buddhists, are now to be found in India. But probably the disappearance of this religion is not to be attributed to persecution only; the orthodox themselves, and especially the Vishnuvies, have made some approximations to the creed of their ancient adversaries, by making Buddha an incarnation of Vishnu, by permitting men of every class to embrace a monastic life, and by abolishing in a great degree the use of bloody sacrifices. Hence it is probable that the remnant of the Buddhists may have been lost in the Jains and Vishnuvies.

It would be inconsistent with the limits of this work to enter into any consideration of the Buddhistic sects, or to describe the modifications which that religion has received from the character of the different nations in which it has been established; still less to pursue the difficult and important inquiry of the effects produced by Buddhism indirectly; but I may be permitted to remark that decisive traces of its influence are to be discovered in the Gnostic heresies that corrupted Christianity, and in the Sufeeism which threatens at no distant day to overthrow Mahomedanism.

CHAPTER XXI.

GOUR.—MUSQUITOES.—A WILD SOW SHOT.

From Bode Gyah we made the best of our way to Patna, where our budgerow was waiting for us, and thence dropped down the river to Rajemah'l. Here we crossed the Ganges, and proceeded in our palankeens to the ruins of Gour, once the capital of Bengal, and about thirty miles from Rajemah'l. The city of Gour was formerly of vast extent, as is evident from the ruins now remaining, which occupy a space of twenty square miles. Several villages stand upon its site; and what may be called the modern town, in which there are eight tolerably good bazaars, contains a population of somewhere about thirty thousand souls.

Nothing scarcely remains of the old city, except a few solemn ruins. One of the gateways is still a magnificent object; it is a noble piece of architecture and majestic even in decay. It originally formed one of the principal entrances into the town. The arch is upwards of fifty feet high, and the wall of immense thickness. The ravages of time are indeed fearfully visible upon it, but it nevertheless appears likely to stand for centuries. This neighbourhood swarms with vermin and reptiles of all kinds, and only two days before our arrival, a boa snake, two-and-twenty feet long, had been killed close by the old gateway. The tanks were so filled with alligators, that it was dangerous to approach their banks. Some of these creatures, however, were so tame as to come at the call of a fakeer, and take rice from his hand.

We found the musquitoes so intolerable, that it was scarcely possible to obtain any rest at night. In fact the whole vicinity has been so neglected, that it has become the resort of everything noxious and disagreeable. The ground is covered with the rankest vegetation, which is permitted to wither and rot upon the surface, so that the place is very unhealthy from the pestilential effluvia continually arising. Though this is an evil easily remedied, still the inhabitants permit it to remain with the greatest unconcern, preferring to be visited with the most frightful distempers, rather than take the trouble to remove the cause of them. The soil is so fertile that it would yield an immense harvest for the labour of cultivation; and yet it is left untilled except a few small patches which return a scanty crop to the niggard toil of several poor farmers, who seek from it a bare subsistence.

The morning after we reached Gour, we went out, as was our usual practice, with our guns, but the jungle was so rank and the swamps so dangerous that we were soon glad to return. On our way back a large wild sow was shot at by Mr. Daniell, and wounded in the hind leg. She was so much disabled that she could not make her escape; but the fierceness of her resistance, even though taken at such a dis-

advantage, was surprising. She turned upon the person who approached to despatch her, with a ferocious activity, her jaws covered with foam, and champing with the most savage aspect of fury. A second shot broke the other hind leg, and she was now quite unable either to advance or retreat; she nevertheless contrived to scramble into a ditch filled with tall jungle grass, which so entirely covered her that we lost sight of her for some time. As we could neither hear her moan nor see her stir, we began to imagine that she was dead and our hope of a griskin defeated. At length a small dog belonging to one of our party roused her from her painful repose, when she inflicted upon the poor little creature a wound so severe as ultimately to cause its death. The grass was now soon plucked up, and the wounded quarry exposed. Although she could offer no effectual resistance, she nevertheless made astonishing efforts to escape, dragging herself forward into the grass, and using incredible exertions to wound her assailants. She literally sprang at them on her two stumps, evincing an indomitable determination not to die unavenged; and it required great agility and caution, on the part of our attendants, to defeat her desperate purpose.

The men attacked her with thick bamboos, and having broken one of her forelegs she was soon despatched. It was now about noon, and, within five hours after, the flesh was in such a state of decomposition that it was impossible to dress it. The heat of the day had been extreme, and the severe bruises which the animal had received from the bamboos of our merciless followers, had so accelerated the natural activity of putrefaction in so warm a climate, that we were obliged to consign her to the vultures, which gladly reaped the fruits of our labours and disappointment.

On the following day we returned to our budgerow, and proceeded leisurely down the Ganges. Not far below Rajemah'l we were overtaken by a severe squall, which had nearly driven us on shore. We did not escape without damage, as our budgerow struck against the bank, and received a severe shock, the water making its way so rapidly into her that we were obliged to keep two men constantly employed in baling her out. Our patilla, or baggage boat, was swamped, and went to the bottom with every thing we possessed in the world, except our papers and drawings, which we happened luckily to have on board the budgerow. The patilla was considerably astern of us when she went down, nor were we conscious of the accident until we had moored for the night, when the boatmen appeared with rueful countenances to report the disaster.

Next morning we proceeded up the river in search of the sunken boat, and at length saw her mast just above water near the opposite shore. It was now clear enough that our baggage had received the benefit of a night's soaking in consecrated water, a blessing which we should have been better satisfied to have dispensed with, as we found the sacred element just as hostile to portmanteaus and hair trunks with their perishable contents, as the waters of the commonest stream.

Having got into a small boat, we made for the spot where the mast was visible, and with the assistance of our dandies succeeded in saving a portion of our things from the wreck, though many were irrecoverable. In the course of the day the budgerow was despatched to our aid, when we put into her those things which we had recovered, and again dropped quietly down the river. The day was beautiful, though the loss of our baggage rendered us less alive to it than we no doubt should have been but for the unlooked-for misfortune of the preceding evening.

Boats are exposed to great danger in coming down the Ganges when the current is strong and the wind high. The wind assisting the impetus of the current frequently drives them with such force against the high banks, already undermined by the water, as to dislodge the superincumbent earth, which immediately falls in immense masses, and unless the boats are instantly driven past by the rapidity of the stream, they are overwhelmed and sunk. The current, however, is generally so rapid at the seasons of the year in which these accidents are to be apprehended, that no sooner do the boats strike than they are borne away beyond the reach of danger. Nevertheless, their progress is sometimes arrested for the moment, when the bank falls upon them, and they are inevitably swamped. While the river is falling, where the stream is impetuous, boats are occasionally thrown with violence against the banks of sand, which greatly interrupt the course of the Ganges, except when it is swollen by the rains and the melting of the mountain snow. Should such an accident occur, a passage must be immediately cleared by human labour, though if the water should be fast subsiding, this is often impracticable; there is then no alternative but to allow the stranded boat to remain through the season upon the shoal, until at the periodical monsoon the water rises sufficiently high to float her.

The evening after our disaster a budgerow, in which was an English officer, passed us on its way to Benares. As we moored near the same spot, he invited us on board his boat. There was spread upon the roof of the cabin the skin of a large tiger which he had killed the preceding day. He told us that as the dandies were preparing to start in the morning, his budgerow being close to the shore, a tiger rushed from a neighbouring covert, and springing into it, seated itself upon the roof of the cabin. The boatmen instantly crept out of sight: the officer loaded his rifle and desired his servant to tie a rope to one of the small beams of the boat and, having first made a running noose, slip the reverse end gently over the animal's tail, which hung down on the outside of the cabin;—this object was therefore easily accomplished. No sooner did the fierce beast feel the pressure of the cord, than it sprang in wild alarm from the cabin-roof, and such was the impetuosity of its spring, that the beam gave way, and, when it gained the shore, was hanging at its tail. The tiger rolled on the bank with pain, writhing and yelling furiously, and the officer, taking a deliberate aim from the cabin-window, shot it dead.

On the morrow we floated again upon the broad bosom of the Ganges, which was hourly widening as we approached Calcutta. As I now call to my recollection the beauties of that magnificent river, I shall indulge myself, and I trust gratify the reader, by giving a poetical description of it from the pen of one of its own native bards.

> "Gold river! gold river! how gallantly now
> Our bark on thy bright breast is lifting her prow!
> In the pride of her beauty how swiftly she flies,
> Like a white-winged spirit through topaz-paved skies!
>
> "Gold river! gold river! thy bosom is calm,
> And o'er thee the breezes are shedding their balm;
> And nature beholds her fair features pourtray'd
> In the glass of thy bosom serenely display'd.
>
> "Gold river! gold river! the sun to thy waves
> Is fleeting to rest in thy cool coral caves;
> And thence, with his tiar of light, in the morn
> He will rise, and the skies with his glory adorn.
>
> "Gold river! gold river! how bright is the beam
> That lightens and crimsons thy soft flowing stream!
> Whose waters beneath make a musical clashing—
> Whose waves as they burst in their brightness are flashing!
>
> "Gold river! gold river! the moon will soon grace
> The hall of the stars with her light-shedding face;
> The wandering planets will over thee throng,
> And seraphs will waken their music and song.
>
> "Gold river! gold river! our brief course is done,
> And safe in the city our home we have won;
> And as to the bright sun, now dropp'd from our view,
> So, Ganga, we bid thee a cheerful adieu!"

These stanzas are taken from a volume of poems written in English by Kasiprasad Ghosh, a young

Hindoo. I am indebted to the kindness of Miss Emma Roberts, a lady of high literary attainments, who knew him in India, for the following particulars.

Kasiprasad Ghosh is of Brahminical descent. His ancestors were distinguished by holding high and responsible appointments under the native rulers of Bengal. Since the occupation of this vast province by the British, they have held a rank equally high as private members of their community. In 1821, when the subject of this brief memoir was fourteen years old, he was sent to the Anglo-Indian college at Calcutta, established under the superintendence of Mr. Horace Hayman Wilson, now Professor of Sanscrit at the University of Oxford. At this period the young Hindoo began to study the English language. During the six years that he was a member of this institution, he distinguished himself by several compositions of great merit, undertaken at the recommendation of Mr. Wilson. A critical essay upon Mill's British India, read at the public examination in 1829, was esteemed so highly creditable to his talents, that the Calcutta Government Gazette printed copious extracts from it, which were subsequently republished in London in the Asiatic Journal. The early productions of Kasiprasad Ghosh now appeared from time to time in the Calcutta periodicals, and the attention they attracted, together with the encomiums bestowed upon them by all who were acquainted with the disadvantages under which their author laboured, induced him to publish a volume of poems: this was exceedingly well received in India, and deservedly so, as the poems evince talent of no common order.

The personal appearance of this interesting Hindoo is highly prepossessing. His countenance is handsome and intellectual, his figure well-proportioned, and set off to great advantage by the graceful costume of his country. He invariably dresses in white muslin of the finest texture, his turban and large sleeves being most elaborately plaited, and the only costly portion of his attire is a splendid Cashmere shawl arranged with that happy taste which Asiatics so well understand how to employ. The young poet is distinguished by an easy and courteous demeanour and a modest estimate of his own acquirements; whilst the anxiety which he manifests to cultivate the acquaintance of foreigners of talent, combined with his own high personal and mental endowments, render the present tribute to his merits an agreeable duty.

CHAPTER XXII.

CALCUTTA.—EDIFICES.—SUNDERBUNDS.

On the fifth day after we quitted Gour we reached Calcutta, from the splendour of its buildings now called the City of Palaces, though within a century it was nothing better than a rude straggling town without regularity or beauty, containing indeed a dense population, and surrounded by a dreary and unwholesome jungle, the haunt of robbers, and the abode of beasts of prey.

The modern town extends above six miles along the eastern bank of the Hoogley, and presents a very animated picture from the river here curving into a large bay, from the opposite side of which, called Garden-house reach, the view is taken represented in the engraving. This reach takes its name from several elegant country houses erected in the neighbourhood, each enclosed by an extensive garden; and here their opulent owners retire after the business of the day is concluded at their offices in the city. The buildings of the European portion of the town present an appearance of great splendour from their almost invariably having extensive and lofty porticos, supported on numerous pillars, which impart an air of Grecian grandeur to those edifices. To persons just arrived from Europe the houses appear very imposing from their novelty of style, their size, and the richness of their architectural embellishments. The squareness and simplicity of their forms is striking, though this simplicity is perhaps too much intruded upon by the gorgeous façades and numerous columns with which they are generally adorned. The absence of chimneys is a novelty that does not escape a European eye, and associates with their grandeur of aspect the idea of a want of comfort rather repugnant to our notions of social enjoyment. The roofs of the houses are invariably terraced and surrounded by handsome balustrades, these being far more light and elegant than a parapet. The windows are large, and instead of being glazed are covered with venetian blinds, in order at once to admit the air and exclude the light, for heat is inseparable from light in this warm climate. The architecture, which is of the Italian school, is well adapted to a tropical country, though in some instances taste has been sacrificed to vulgar whim, many of the private dwellings having two pediments, as if, because one formed an elegant finish, two must give a proportionate increase of magnificence to the structure.

There is a square within the city extending upwards of a quarter of a mile each way, in the centre of which is a large tank surrounded by a low wall, and protected by an elegant iron railing. The top of the wall is at least fifty feet above the level of the water, to which there is a descent by a broad handsome flight of steps.

As rain water is much used in Calcutta for domestic and culinary purposes, there is set apart in every house a room, in which is a number of large earthen jars. These are filled from the terraced roofs during the monsoons, and the water is preserved by an infusion of charcoal pounded small and thrown into each jar, which, by arresting the process of putrefaction, keeps the water sweet for any reasonable period.

The most striking edifice in Calcutta is the Government house. The lower story forms a handsome solid basement, with arcades on every side. All the pillars are of the Ionic order, though one of the largest rooms in the building is supported by Doric columns so beautifully chunamed as to resemble the finest white marble. There are four wings, one at each corner of the house, connected by circular passages, by which means there is a free circulation of air all round. These wings contain the private apartments, the main structure being devoted to the several public rooms set apart for the despatch of Government business, and for those public entertainments for which the metropolis of British India has been long distinguished in the palace of her rulers.

There are only two English churches in this large city, one of which appears in the engraving. It is a graceful structure, built by an officer of engineers, and does him great credit, as he has displayed a refined taste in the disposal of its architectural features. The other church is a much plainer building, and altogether inferior. Although from Garden-house reach the city has an air of grandeur unequalled by any native town in India, it must nevertheless be confessed that

at Delhi, Agra, and Lucknow, there are edifices of a far superior order in point of architecture, than the finest at Calcutta, and which indeed may fairly challenge comparison with anything of a similar kind in Europe.

Next to the Government house the principal building is the Custom-house, a low but capacious edifice with an elegant front, and containing extensive and commodious warerooms. At Cheringhee, the fashionable part of the town, there is a line of magnificent houses, extending like a row of palaces, and almost realizing some of the fictions of Eastern splendour. These houses are all inhabited by Europeans. They are mostly stuccoed, and stand each within a large area, being well ventilated; nor indeed is there wanting anything which the greatest refinement in luxury can suggest to remove the inconveniences of climate, and render them delightful abodes.

Although the portion of Calcutta inhabited by Europeans is airy, attractive, and imposing, nothing can exceed the wretchedness of that part of it occupied by natives. The streets are narrow, dirty, and unpaved. The great proportion of houses are little better than mud hovels, swarming with a squalid, half-starved, miserable population. Here disease, that constant ally of poverty and privation, is perpetually raging, and thousands are yearly victims to the awful evils thus superinduced to the miseries of destitution; nor does there appear any prospect of amelioration to those wretched beings who crowd together in the suburbs of this vast metropolis, only to form a sad community of wretchedness. While the cholera prevailed, seven hundred daily are said to have fallen victims to this terrible scourge for a period of many weeks, during which time enjoyment of all kinds seemed suspended, and not an hour passed in which the wail of lamentation for the dead did not remind the living of the desolation that was spreading around them.

Fort William, standing about four or five hundred yards below the city, is a place of great strength. From the city a road runs by the river in front of the fort to Garden-house reach, round the shore of the bay, a distance of at least three miles, and from this point the best general views of Calcutta are obtained. The citadel towards the water, by which the only approach can be made with any reasonable prospect of success, has the form of a large salient angle, the faces of which enfilade the course of the river. The ditch is dry, with a reservoir in the middle, that receives the water of the Hoogley by means of two sluices protected by the fort. The citadel was commenced by Lord Clive after the battle of Plassey. It is capable of accommodating a garrison of fifteen thousand men, and the works are so extensive that at least ten thousand would be required to defend them efficiently. They are said to have cost the Company upwards of two millions sterling. The interior of the fort is perfectly open, presenting to the view large grass plats and gravel walks, kept cool by rows of trees all in the finest order and fullest vigour of their growth, intermixed with piles of balls, bombshells, and cannon. Between the town and fort is the esplanade, a fine level, where the inhabitants enjoy a refreshing ride "at shut of even," when a grateful breeze from the river generally prevails, cooling the body and imparting an elasticity to the spirits altogether delightful.

The Hoogley exhibits at all times a very animated scene, but more especially at flood tide, when vessels from all parts of the world, and of every size and form, cover the broad bosom of its majestic stream. Indiamen of six hundred tons are frequently seen at anchor off Calcutta. A remarkable peculiarity of this river is that sudden influx of the tide called the bore, which rises in a huge wave sometimes to the height of sixteen or eighteen feet, sweeping up the stream at the rate of seventeen miles an hour, and overwhelming all the small craft within its rapid flow. It runs on the Calcutta side, but seldom extends above one-fourth part across the river, so that the shipping are generally beyond the reach of its influence. It nevertheless at times causes such an agitation that the largest vessels at anchor nearer the opposite shore pitch and roll with considerable violence.

One eminent advantage that Calcutta possesses is its inland navigation, which renders it the emporium of a vast variety of foreign imports; these are conveyed on the Ganges and its subsidiary streams to the northern parts of Hindostan, which return their commercial produce to the capital through the same channels. The amount of property commonly kept on sale by the native merchants is incredible;—the article of cloth alone has been estimated at a million sterling on the average. From the great variety of merchandise brought to this city, the property afloat is perhaps seldom less than eighteen or twenty million sterling, though it is probable that the late large failures, by paralysing the monied and commercial interests, have considerably abridged this prodigious flux of capital. In 1808 the Calcutta Government bank was established. Fifty lacs of rupees—about five hundred thousand pounds—were advanced by the Government and private speculators, both native and European; forty lacs, or four hundred thousand pounds, belonging to the latter, and ten lacs, or a hundred thousand pounds, to the former.

Calcutta has undergone great improvements and is much enlarged within the last fifty years. The blackhole, the monument erected by Mr. Holwell to commemorate the horrible cruelty of Sevajee ud Dowlah who, having captured the British capital of Bengal, shut up a hundred and forty-six prisoners in a dismal cellar twenty feet square, in which all perished except twenty-three—the old Government house and several other buildings which existed a half century ago exist no more. The city has been mostly added to on the eastern bank of the river. Govinda Ram Mittee's pagoda, I believe, still stands; it is an extensive pile of peculiar form, and though partaking of none of the higher beauties of Hindoo architecture, is nevertheless a structure of much beauty. It was formerly, I believe, a place of great sanctity, though now no longer resorted to but by a few of the lower castes.

The inhabitants of Calcutta, native and European, are computed at about six hundred thousand souls, and the immediate neighbourhood within a circuit of twenty miles is supposed to contain a population of nearly two millions and half.

Just before sunrise the air is cool and refreshing; it is therefore the custom to rise early and take a ride before breakfast, which is ready about nine. At halfpast one o'clock tiffin, or luncheon, is served, and dinner at sunset. The wines chiefly drunk are Madeira and claret. The tables are served with a variety of game, partridges, quails, peafowl, wild ducks, ortolans, hares, and venison. Fruits are to be had in great profusion and exceedingly cheap. But the chief luxury at Calcutta is the mango fish, so called from its only appearing during the mango season, and which is not approached in delicacy of flavour by any fish known in Europe. The style in which civilians live can scarcely be imagined by any one who has not crossed the Indian ocean. Even young writers affect such an air of state, and keep such expensive establishments, that notwithstanding their liberal allowances they often become so deeply involved as to be ever after unable to release themselves from the incumbrance.

Nearly a hundred miles below Calcutta, at the embouchure of the Hoogley, is the delta of the Ganges, called the Sunderbunds, composed of a labyrinth of streams and creeks, all of which are salt, except those that communicate immediately with the principal arm of the sacred river; those numerous canals being so disposed, as to form a complete inland navigation.

A few years before our visit to Calcutta, the captain of a country ship, while passing the Sunderbunds, sent a boat into one of the creeks to obtain some fresh fruits which are cultivated by the few miserable inhabitants of this inhospitable region. Having reached the shore the crew moored the boat under a bank, and left one of their party to take care of her. During their absence, the lascar, who remained in charge of the boat, overcome by heat, lay down under the seats and fell asleep. Whilst he was in this happy state of unconsciousness, an enormous boa-constrictor emerged from the jungle, reached the boat, had already coiled its huge body round the sleeper, and was in the very act of crushing him to death, when his companions fortunately returned at this auspicious moment, and attacking the monster severed a portion of its tail, which so disabled it that it no longer retained the power of doing mischief. The snake was then easily despatched, and found to measure sixty-two feet and some inches in length.* The immense size of these snakes has been frequently called in question, but I know not why it should when the fact has been authenticated by so many eye-witnesses. Nor was it unknown to ancient historians; for Suetonius, in the forty third chapter of his Lives of the first Twelve Cæsars, mentions that the Emperor Augustus over and above the regular shows, gave others occasionally for the purpose of exhibiting any extraordinary object of which he might have

* The original picture, painted by Mr. W. Daniell, is in the possession of le Baron de Noual de la Loyrie; and that of the "Favourite of the Harem," also by the same artist, is the property of R. W. Cox, Esq. of Lawford, Essex.

www.bookjungle.com *email: sales@bookjungle.com fax: 630-214-0564 mail: Book Jungle PO Box 2226 Champaign, IL 61825*

The Codes Of Hammurabi And Moses
W. W. Davies

QTY

The discovery of the Hammurabi Code is one of the greatest achievements of archaeology, and is of paramount interest, not only to the student of the Bible, but also to all those interested in ancient history...

Religion ISBN: *1-59462-338-4* Pages:132 MSRP $12.95

The Theory of Moral Sentiments
Adam Smith

QTY

This work from 1749. contains original theories of conscience amd moral judgment and it is the foundation for systemof morals.

Philosophy ISBN: *1-59462-777-0* Pages:536 MSRP $19.95

Jessica's First Prayer
Hesba Stretton

QTY

In a screened and secluded corner of one of the many railway-bridges which span the streets of London there could be seen a few years ago, from five o'clock every morning until half past eight, a tidily set-out coffee-stall, consisting of a trestle and board, upon which stood two large tin cans, with a small fire of charcoal burning under each so as to keep the coffee boiling during the early hours of the morning when the work-people were thronging into the city on their way to their daily toil...

Childrens ISBN: *1-59462-373-2* Pages:84 MSRP $9.95

My Life and Work
Henry Ford

QTY

Henry Ford revolutionized the world with his implementation of mass production for the Model T automobile. Gain valuable business insight into his life and work with his own auto-biography... "We have only started on our development of our country we have not as yet, with all our talk of wonderful progress, done more than scratch the surface. The progress has been wonderful enough but..."

Biographies/ ISBN: *1-59462-198-5* Pages:300 MSRP $21.95

www.bookjungle.com *email: sales@bookjungle.com fax: 630-214-0564 mail: Book Jungle PO Box 2226 Champaign, IL 61825*

The Art of Cross-Examination
Francis Wellman

QTY

I presume it is the experience of every author, after his first book is published upon an important subject, to be almost overwhelmed with a wealth of ideas and illustrations which could readily have been included in his book, and which to his own mind, at least, seem to make a second edition inevitable. Such certainly was the case with me; and when the first edition had reached its sixth impression in five months, I rejoiced to learn that it seemed to my publishers that the book had met with a sufficiently favorable reception to justify a second and considerably enlarged edition. ..

Reference   ISBN: *1-59462-647-2*   Pages:412 MSRP *$19.95*

On the Duty of Civil Disobedience
Henry David Thoreau

QTY

Thoreau wrote his famous essay, On the Duty of Civil Disobedience, as a protest against an unjust but popular war and the immoral but popular institution of slave-owning. He did more than write—he declined to pay his taxes, and was hauled off to gaol in consequence. Who can say how much this refusal of his hastened the end of the war and of slavery ?

Law   ISBN: *1-59462-747-9*   Pages:48 MSRP *$7.45*

Dream Psychology Psychoanalysis for Beginners
Sigmund Freud

QTY

Sigmund Freud, born Sigismund Schlomo Freud (May 6, 1856 - September 23, 1939), was a Jewish-Austrian neurologist and psychiatrist who co-founded the psychoanalytic school of psychology. Freud is best known for his theories of the unconscious mind, especially involving the mechanism of repression; his redefinition of sexual desire as mobile and directed towards a wide variety of objects; and his therapeutic techniques, especially his understanding of transference in the therapeutic relationship and the presumed value of dreams as sources of insight into unconscious desires.

Psychology   ISBN: *1-59462-905-6*   Pages:196 MSRP *$15.45*

The Miracle of Right Thought
Orison Swett Marden

QTY

Believe with all of your heart that you will do what you were made to do. When the mind has once formed the habit of holding cheerful, happy, prosperous pictures, it will not be easy to form the opposite habit. It does not matter how improbable or how far away this realization may see, or how dark the prospects may be, if we visualize them as best we can, as vividly as possible, hold tenaciously to them and vigorously struggle to attain them, they will gradually become actualized, realized in the life. But a desire, a longing without endeavor, a yearning abandoned or held indifferently will vanish without realization.

Self Help   ISBN: *1-59462-644-8*   Pages:360 MSRP *$25.45*

www.bookjungle.com *email: sales@bookjungle.com fax: 630-214-0564 mail: Book Jungle PO Box 2226 Champaign, IL 61825*
QTY

	Title	ISBN	Price
☐	**The Rosicrucian Cosmo-Conception Mystic Christianity** *by Max Heindel* *The Rosicrucian Cosmo-conception is not dogmatic, neither does it appeal to any other authority than the reason of the student. It is: not controversial, but is: sent forth in the, hope that it may help to clear...*	ISBN: *1-59462-188-8*	**$38.95** *New Age/Religion Pages 646*
☐	**Abandonment To Divine Providence** *by Jean-Pierre de Caussade* *"The Rev. Jean Pierre de Caussade was one of the most remarkable spiritual writers of the Society of Jesus in France in the 18th Century. His death took place at Toulouse in 1751. His works have gone through many editions and have been republished..."*	ISBN: *1-59462-228-0*	**$25.95** *Inspirational/Religion Pages 400*
☐	**Mental Chemistry** *by Charles Haanel* *Mental Chemistry allows the change of material conditions by combining and appropriately utilizing the power of the mind. Much like applied chemistry creates something new and unique out of careful combinations of chemicals the mastery of mental chemistry...*	ISBN: *1-59462-192-6*	**$23.95** *New Age Pages 354*
☐	**The Letters of Robert Browning and Elizabeth Barret Barrett 1845-1846 vol II** *by Robert Browning and Elizabeth Barrett*	ISBN: *1-59462-193-4*	**$35.95** *Biographies Pages 596*
☐	**Gleanings In Genesis (volume I)** *by Arthur W. Pink* *Appropriately has Genesis been termed "the seed plot of the Bible" for in it we have, in germ form, almost all of the great doctrines which are afterwards fully developed in the books of Scripture which follow...*	ISBN: *1-59462-130-6*	**$27.45** *Religion/Inspirational Pages 420*
☐	**The Master Key** *by L. W. de Laurence* *In no branch of human knowledge has there been a more lively increase of the spirit of research during the past few years than in the study of Psychology, Concentration and Mental Discipline. The requests for authentic lessons in Thought Control, Mental Discipline and...*	ISBN: *1-59462-001-6*	**$30.95** *New Age/Business Pages 422*
☐	**The Lesser Key Of Solomon Goetia** *by L. W. de Laurence* *This translation of the first book of the "Lemegton" which is now for the first time made accessible to students of Talismanic Magic was done, after careful collation and edition, from numerous Ancient Manuscripts in Hebrew, Latin, and French...*	ISBN: *1-59462-092-X*	**$9.95** *New Age/Occult Pages 92*
☐	**Rubaiyat Of Omar Khayyam** *by Edward Fitzgerald* *Edward Fitzgerald, whom the world has already learned, in spite of his own efforts to remain within the shadow of anonymity, to look upon as one of the rarest poets of the century, was born at Bredfield, in Suffolk, on the 31st of March, 1809. He was the third son of John Purcell...*	ISBN: *1-59462-332-5*	**$13.95** *Music Pages 172*
☐	**Ancient Law** *by Henry Maine* *The chief object of the following pages is to indicate some of the earliest ideas of mankind, as they are reflected in Ancient Law, and to point out the relation of those ideas to modern thought.*	ISBN: *1-59462-128-4*	**$29.95** *Religion/History Pages 452*
☐	**Far-Away Stories** *by William J. Locke* *"Good wine needs no bush, but a collection of mixed vintages does. And this book is just such a collection. Some of the stories I do not want to remain buried for ever in the museum files of dead magazine-numbers an author's not unpardonable vanity..."*	ISBN: *1-59462-129-2*	**$19.45** *Fiction Pages 272*
☐	**Life of David Crockett** *by David Crockett* *"Colonel David Crockett was one of the most remarkable men of the times in which he lived. Born in humble life, but gifted with a strong will, an indomitable courage, and unremitting perseverance..."*	ISBN: *1-59462-250-7*	**$27.45** *Biographies/New Age Pages 424*
☐	**Lip-Reading** *by Edward Nitchie* *Edward B. Nitchie, founder of the New York School for the Hard of Hearing, now the Nitchie School of Lip-Reading, Inc, wrote "LIP-READING Principles and Practice". The development and perfecting of this meritorious work on lip-reading was an undertaking...*	ISBN: *1-59462-206-X*	**$25.95** *How-to Pages 400*
☐	**A Handbook of Suggestive Therapeutics, Applied Hypnotism, Psychic Science** *by Henry Munro*	ISBN: *1-59462-214-0*	**$24.95** *Health/New Age/Health/Self-help Pages 376*
☐	**A Doll's House: and Two Other Plays** *by Henrik Ibsen* *Henrik Ibsen created this classic when in revolutionary 1848 Rome. Introducing some striking concepts in playwriting for the realist genre, this play has been studied the world over.*	ISBN: *1-59462-112-8*	**$19.95** *Fiction/Classics/Plays 308*
☐	**The Light of Asia** *by sir Edwin Arnold* *In this poetic masterpiece, Edwin Arnold describes the life and teachings of Buddha. The man who was to become known as Buddha to the world was born as Prince Gautama of India but he rejected the worldly riches and abandoned the reigns of power when...*	ISBN: *1-59462-204-3*	**$13.95** *Religion/History/Biographies Pages 170*
☐	**The Complete Works of Guy de Maupassant** *by Guy de Maupassant* *"For days and days, nights and nights, I had dreamed of that first kiss which was to consecrate our engagement, and I knew not on what spot I should put my lips..."*	ISBN: *1-59462-157-8*	**$16.95** *Fiction/Classics Pages 240*
☐	**The Art of Cross-Examination** *by Francis L. Wellman* *Written by a renowned trial lawyer, Wellman imparts his experience and uses case studies to explain how to use psychology to extract desired information through questioning.*	ISBN: *1-59462-309-0*	**$26.95** *How-to/Science/Reference Pages 408*
☐	**Answered or Unanswered?** *by Louisa Vaughan* *Miracles of Faith in China*	ISDN: *1-59462-248-5*	**$10.95** *Religion Pages 112*
☐	**The Edinburgh Lectures on Mental Science (1909)** *by Thomas* *This book contains the substance of a course of lectures recently given by the writer in the Queen Street Hall, Edinburgh. Its purpose is to indicate the Natural Principles governing the relation between Mental Action and Material Conditions...*	ISBN: *1-59462-008-3*	**$11.95** *New Age/Psychology Pages 148*
☐	**Ayesha** *by H. Rider Haggard* *Verily and indeed it is the unexpected that happens! Probably if there was one person upon the earth from whom the Editor of this, and of a certain previous history, did not expect to hear again...*	ISBN: *1-59462-301-5*	**$24.95** *Classics Pages 380*
☐	**Ayala's Angel** *by Anthony Trollope* *The two girls were both pretty, but Lucy who was twenty-one who supposed to be simple and comparatively unattractive, whereas Ayala was credited, as her Bombwhat romantic name might show, with poetic charm and a taste for romance. Ayala when her father died was nineteen...*	ISBN: *1-59462-352-X*	**$29.95** *Fiction Pages 484*
☐	**The American Commonwealth** *by James Bryce* *An interpretation of American democratic political theory. It examines political mechanics and society from the perspective of Scotsman James Bryce*	ISBN: *1-59462-286-8*	**$34.45** *Politics Pages 572*
☐	**Stories of the Pilgrims** *by Margaret P. Pumphrey* *This book explores pilgrims religious oppression in England as well as their escape to Holland and eventual crossing to America on the Mayflower, and their early days in New England...*	ISBN: *1-59462-116-0*	**$17.95** *History Pages 268*

www.bookjungle.com email: sales@bookjungle.com fax: 630-214-0564 mail: Book Jungle PO Box 2226 Champaign, IL 61825

QTY

The Fasting Cure *by Sinclair Upton* ISBN: *1-59462-222-1* **$13.95**
In the Cosmopolitan Magazine for May, 1910, and in the Contemporary Review (London) for April, 1910, I published an article dealing with my experiences in fasting. I have written a great many magazine articles, but never one which attracted so much attention... New Age/Self Help/Health Pages 164

Hebrew Astrology *by Sepharial* ISBN: *1-59462-308-2* **$13.45**
In these days of advanced thinking it is a matter of common observation that we have left many of the old landmarks behind and that we are now pressing forward to greater heights and to a wider horizon than that which represented the mind-content of our progenitors... Astrology Pages 144

Thought Vibration or The Law of Attraction in the Thought World ISBN: *1-59462-127-6* **$12.95**
by William Walker Atkinson Psychology/Religion Pages 144

Optimism *by Helen Keller* ISBN: *1-59462-108-X* **$15.95**
Helen Keller was blind, deaf, and mute since 19 months old, yet famously learned how to overcome these handicaps, communicate with the world, and spread her lectures promoting optimism. An inspiring read for everyone... Biographies/Inspirational Pages 84

Sara Crewe *by Frances Burnett* ISBN: *1-59462-360-0* **$9.45**
In the first place, Miss Minchin lived in London. Her home was a large, dull, tall one, in a large, dull square, where all the houses were alike, and all the sparrows were alike, and where all the door-knockers made the same heavy sound... Childrens/Classic Pages 88

The Autobiography of Benjamin Franklin *by Benjamin Franklin* ISBN: *1-59462-135-7* **$24.95**
The Autobiography of Benjamin Franklin has probably been more extensively read than any other American historical work, and no other book of its kind has had such ups and downs of fortune. Franklin lived for many years in England, where he was agent... Biographies/History Pages 332

Name	
Email	
Telephone	
Address	
City, State ZIP	

☐ Credit Card   ☐ Check / Money Order

Credit Card Number	
Expiration Date	
Signature	

Please Mail to: Book Jungle
PO Box 2226
Champaign, IL 61825
or Fax to: 630-214-0564

ORDERING INFORMATION

web: *www.bookjungle.com*
email: *sales@bookjungle.com*
fax: *630-214-0564*
mail: *Book Jungle PO Box 2226 Champaign, IL 61825*
or PayPal *to sales@bookjungle.com*

Please contact us for bulk discounts

DIRECT-ORDER TERMS

**20% Discount if You Order
Two or More Books**
Free Domestic Shipping!
Accepted: Master Card, Visa,
Discover, American Express

www.ingramcontent.com/pod-product-compliance
Lightning Source LLC
Chambersburg PA
CBHW081831170426
43199CB00017B/2694